D1233607

UNIVERSITY OF CALIFORNIA
BIBLIOGRAPHIC GUIDES

SERIAL MUSIC

A Classified Bibliography
of Writings on Twelve-Tone
and Electronic Music

by ANN PHILLIPS BASART

1961

UNIVERSITY OF CALIFORNIA PRESS

BERKELEY AND LOS ANGELES

University of California Press
Berkeley and Los Angeles, California

Cambridge University Press
London, England

© 1961 by The Regents of the University of California

Library of Congress Catalog Card Number: 61-7538

Manufactured in the United States of America

In Memoriam E.S.S.

PREFACE

The twelve-tone technique, once thought to be the private and unintelligible musical language of a small group of composers, is today one of the most important influences in European and American music. Although it still creates a great deal of controversy, and although it has not yet been widely accepted by the general public, dodecaphony has achieved a permanent status in the history of music.

"Schönberg is not yet in 'Grove' (1910), and the notices in other works of reference are infinitesimal," wrote Charles Maclean in an early article on Schoenberg. Today the situation has changed so much that not only is Schoenberg in Grove's Dictionary, but articles and books about him, the twelve-tone technique, and other composers who use the technique continue to be written at an ever-increasing rate.

Because of this great body of writing, it is difficult for anyone interested in serial music to know where to begin. A few related bibliographies have appeared to date, but none so far with the purpose and scope of the present work. The most extensive bibliographies on Schoenberg, Berg, and Webern have appeared in René Leibowitz's Schoenberg and his school (1949), Luigi Rognoni's Espressionismo e dodecafonia (1954), Josef Rufer's Composition with twelve notes (1954), and George Perle's dissertation, Serial composition and atonality (1956; revised edition, University of California Press, 1961). Rognoni and Rufer list unpublished writings by these composers on a variety of topics—important information that is outside the scope of the present work.

Donald Mitchell has compiled a selective bibliography that lists writings on twelve-tone music and composers (Hinrichsen's Musical yearbook, 1952), but he does not indicate the contents of these writings. Since his list is taken from secondary sources, the bibliographical information offered varies widely and is in many cases quite scanty. Helmut Kirchmeyer's book, Igor Strawinsky (1958), contains a lengthy bibliography on contemporary music which includes some entries on serial music and composers.

Appearing too late for inclusion in the present work is a bibliography of books and articles on experimental music, compiled by Célestin Deliège and printed in the Revue Belge de musicologie [Special issue on experimental music], 8:136-148 (1959). It is preceded (p. 132-136) by an excellent discussion of the writings of the most important authors in the field. The bibliography is alphabetically arranged within each of the following categories: "Ouvrages," "Articles," "Témoignages d'écrivains," "Divers," and "Ouvrages et articles relatifs à l'électroacoustique musicale." It is principally concerned with the European avant-garde.

Other lists have appeared from time to time in periodical articles and in chapters of specialized books. Most of these are quite brief, and none indicates contents.

The present work is an attempt to gather together a large number of the significant writings—philosophical, historical, and analytical—which have appeared on serial music, and to arrange them by subject. "Serial music" is used in a wide sense here, because this bibliography includes not only twelve-tone music and electronic music (a very recent development, growing out of serial techniques), but also touches upon such related fields as musical expressionism, pre-dodecaphonic atonality, musique concrète, and "chance" music.

The bibliography is arranged in a classified manner, with entries under each topic subarranged chronologically. There are an author index and a subject index. Almost every entry is followed by a brief annotation, indicating the contents, scope, and/or general idea of the book or article. The present work is not, however, a critical bibliography, and, although an attempt has been made to guide the reader by means of the annotations, the quality of the material listed varies rather widely.

Ann P. Basart

CONTENTS

[ix]

INTRODUCTION

ARRANGEMENT

The bibliography is divided into four main sections:

1. Twelve-tone music
2. Electronic music
3. The Viennese school (Schoenberg, Berg, Webern)

These three sections have a classified arrangement.

4. Other composers who use serial techniques

This section is arranged alphabetically by composer.

The topics into which each section is divided are listed in the table of contents. All the entries under each topic are arranged chronologically. Where books and periodicals have the same year of publication, the books are listed first and the periodicals follow by months. Each entry is given in full only once, under the topic it most closely fits. Cross-references refer the user to related entries under other topics; they are arranged chronologically in with the entries.

FORM OF ENTRY

Articles

Entry for an article in a periodical:

491   Mantelli, Alberto. "Note su Alban Berg," Rass mus 9:117-132 (Apr 1936). Mus.

This article by Mantelli will be found in the periodical Rassegna musicale (see the list of abbreviations, p. xiii) in volume 9, pages 117-132, for April 1936. There are musical examples.

Entry for an article in a book:

296   Stefan, Paul. "Arnold Schoenberg" in Thompson, Oscar, ed. Great modern composers. New York, Dodd, Mead, 1941, p. 267-277.

Stefan's article is one of several in Thompson's book, and will be found on pages 267-277.

Books

Monographs

448a Wörner, Karl H. Gotteswort und Magie: die Oper 'Moses und Aron'
      von Arnold Schönberg. Heidelberg, Lambert Schneider, 1959. 93 p.
      Mus., port.

Wörner's book, Gotteswort und Magie: die Oper 'Moses und Aron' von
Arnold Schönberg, was published in Heidelberg by Schneider in 1959, has 93
pages and includes some musical examples and a portrait (of Schoenberg).

Collections

168   Junge Komponisten. Wien, Universal Edition [c1958]. 133 p. Diagrs.,
      mus., tables. (Die Reihe: Information über serielle Musik, 4.)

The title of this book is Junge Komponisten, published in 1958 by Universal
Edition in Vienna. It has 133 pages and contains diagrams, musical examples,
and tables. It is the fourth publication in the series, Die Reihe. (Because all
the articles in the collection are relevant to the subject of this bibliography,
they are listed in detail after the entry, and also will be found in the author
index.)

Cross-references

See no. 89 (Reich, Willi. "Versuch einer Geschichte der Zwölftonmusik" in
      Alte und neue Musik. 1952).

This particular cross-reference, found under the general works on
Arnold Schoenberg, refers the user back to Reich's article, which is
listed in full under the history of twelve-tone music. For a general
explanation of the cross-reference system, see "Arrangement," above.

TO USE THE BIBLIOGRAPHY

If you wish to find all the writings on one topic:
      Consult the table of contents (p. ix-x) if the topic is a broad one (such as
      "history of twelve-tone music," "Boulez—compositional techniques,"
      or "Schoenberg—biography").
      Consult the subject index (p. 147-151) if the topic is more specialized
      (e.g., "Italy—twelve-tone composition," "Indeterminacy in musical
      composition," "Marxist criticisms of twelve-tone music," "Permuta-
      tion of serial elements," or "Combinatoriality").
If you wish to locate all the writings by one author that are included in this
      bibliography, use the author index (p. 129-146).
If you want analyses and discussions of a particular composition, look up
      the composer in the table of contents; his works will be listed in alpha-
      betical order at the end of his section. Individual compositions are not
      included in the subject index.
If you know the title of a book that has no author (e.g., Der blaue Reiter),
      but do not know what subject to look under, use the author index; some
      title entries are included there.

Note: An asterisk (*) indicates an item not seen; bibliographical information for these items has been taken from the Union Catalog at the Library
of the University of California, Berkeley.

ABBREVIATIONS

BAMS	American Musicological Society Bulletin
diagr.	diagram
Dt Univ Zt	Deutsche Universitätszeitung [Göttingen]
I.S.C.M.	International Society for Contemporary Music
JAMS	American Musicological Society Journal
l.	leaf, leaves (i.e., typewritten pages)
M & L	Music and letters
M.G.G.	Die Musik in Geschichte und Gegenwart
Mo mus rec	Monthly musical record
MQ	Musical quarterly
ms.	measure, measures
MT	Musical times
mus.	musical example(s) included in the text
Mus rev	The music review
Mus sur	Music survey
Notes	Music Library Association Notes
NZfM	Neue Zeitschrift für Musik [formerly ZfM]
ÖMZ	Öesterreichische Musik Zeitschrift
op.	opus, opera
p.	page, pages
PAMS	American Musicological Society Papers
port.	portrait
Rass mus	Rassegna musicale
Rev mus	Revue musicale
Riv mus ital	Rivista musicale italiana
RMA Proc	Royal Musical Association Proceedings
Schw MZ	Schweizerische Musikzeitung
Score	The score and I.M.A. magazine
v.	volume, volumes
ZfM	Zeitschrift für Musik [now NZfM]

I

TWELVE-TONE MUSIC

PHILOSOPHY AND CRITICISM

1   Busoni, Ferruccio Benvenuto. Entwurf einer neuen Ästhetik der Tonkunst. 2., erweiterte Ausg. Leipzig, Insel-verlag [1916]. 48 p.
    Post-Wagnerian aesthetics. Discussion of new subdivisions of the
    octave.

See no. 128   (Eimert, Herbert. Atonale Musiklehre, 1924).

2   Tiessen, Heinz. Zur Geschichte der jüngsten Musik (1913-1928).
Mainz, Schotts Söhne [c1928]. 91 p.
    Partial contents: "Expressionismus," p. 39-42; "Schönberg," p. 44-
    46, et passim.
    Aesthetics of the music of 1913-1928.

3   Adorno, Theodor Wiesengrund. "Zur Zwölftontechnik," Anbruch 11:
290-294 (Sept/Oct 1929).
    General considerations of the twelve-tone technique: its audibility;
    whether it is mathematical. Largely a discussion of Schoenberg.

4   Berg, Alban. "What is atonality?" in Slonimsky, Nicolas. Music
since 1900. 3d ed., rev. and enl. New York, Coleman-Ross, 1949,
p. 671-677.
    A translation by M. D. H. Norton from a radio talk given by
    Berg on the Vienna Rundfunk, April 23, 1930.
    Italian translation in Rognoni, p. 290-303 (see no. 94).
    First published as "Was ist Atonal?" in 23, eine wiener Musik-
    zeitschrift, no. 26/27 (June 8, 1936).

5   Pacque, Désiré. "L'atonalité, ou mode chromatique unique," Rev mus
11:135-140 (Aug/Sept 1930).
    The nature of "atonality"; not a new concept.

6   Reich, Willi. "Grenzgebiete der neuen Töne," Die Musik 25:120-123
(Nov 1932).
    "Der Weg zur Komposition in zwölf Tönen," p. 122-123.

7   Sessions, Roger. "Music in crisis: some notes on recent music
history," Modern music 10:63-78 (Jan/Feb 1933).
    Discussion of the aesthetics of the twelve-tone system, p. 70-73.
    Also appears in no. 295 (Armitage, ed., p. 9-39).

8   Lissa, Zofja. "Geschichtliche Vorform der Zwölftontechnik," Acta
musicologica 7:15-21 (Jan/Mar 1935).
    Scriabine's music as a forerunner of 12-tone principles.

9   Gray, Cecil. "Atonalism" in his Predicaments: or music and the future. London, Oxford University Press, 1936, p. 168-195.
General essay discussing Schoenberg, Berg, and Webern.

10   Krenek, Ernst. Über neue Musik: sechs Verlesungen zur Einführung in die theoretischen Grundlagen. Wien, Ringbuchhandlung, 1937. 108 p. Mus.
Six lectures given by Krenek in Vienna in 1936. Partial contents: "Zwölftontechnik," p. 51-70; "Musik und Mathematik," p. 71-89 (discusses various types of rows, including all-interval rows).
Important and lengthy review by Roger Sessions in Modern Music 15:123-128 (Jan/Feb 1938).

11   Krenek, Ernst. Music here and now. Tr. by Barthold Flees. New York, Norton [c1939]. 306 p.
An English translation of no. 10, with added material. Tries to show that atonality and the twelve-tone technique were inevitable developments of Western music, and are the only "music of the future."

12   Sackville-West, Edward. "Atonalism: second thoughts," New statesman and nation [ser. 2] 23:192 (Mar 21, 1942).
A re-evaluation of the importance of atonality and the twelve-tone technique.

See no. 317 (Taylor, Noel H. "Arnold Schoenberg," autumn 1944).

See no. 137 (Eschman, Karl. Changing forms in modern music, 1945).

13   Adorno, Theodor Wiesegrund. Philosophie der neuen Musik. Tübingen, J. C. B. Mohr, 1949, vii + 144 p.
"Schönberg und der Fortschritt," p. 19-88.
Discusses expressionism, form, rhythm, harmony, instrumentation, counterpoint in relation to the twelve-tone technique. Cites works of Berg, Schoenberg, and Webern. No musical examples. (See no. 342.)

14   Koechlin, Charles. "Quelques réflexions au sujet de la musique atonale," Music today [Journal of the I. S. C. M.] 1:26-33 (1949).
Résumé in English, p. 33-35.
Contrasts atonality, which he finds acceptable, with the twelve-tone technique, which he calls unmusical and academic.

See no. 84 (Leibowitz, René. Schoenberg and his school, 1949).

15   "Open forum: variations on a theme. Music's future: tonal or atonal?" Music today [Journal of the I. S. C. M.] 1:132-152 (1949).
Statements answering "Why do you believe or not believe that atonal music will be the music of the future?" by Schoenberg, Berg, Milhaud, Poulenc, Leibowitz, Searle, and other composers.

See no. 325 (Salazar, Adolfo. "Arnold Schoenberg post-mortem," 1951).

See no. 86 (Stuckenschmidt, Hans Heinz. Neue Musik, 1951).

16   Burnier, Lucien. "Réflexions sur la dodécaphonie," Schw MZ 91:14-17 (Jan 1951). Mus.
On dodecaphony as a means of composition rather than as an intellectual exercise.

17   Krenek, Ernst. "Die Zwölftonmusik als Lehre," Melos 18:141-143
      (May 1951).
      A discussion of the literature on twelve-tone theory, particularly
      Eimert's Lehrbuch der Zwölftontechnik (see no. 142).

18   Eimert, Herbert. "Ist Zwölftonmusik lehrbar?" Melos 18:249-251
      (Sept 1951).
      On the difficulties of teaching the twelve-tone technique.

19   Krüger, Walther. "Zwölftonmusik und Gegenwart," Musica 5:503-505
      (Dec 1951).
      The twelve-tone technique as a positive phenomenon. Comments
      on Eimert's Lehrbuch (see no. 142).

20   Hall, Richard. "Twelve-tone music and tradition," Hinrichsen's
      Musical yearbook 7:128-134 (1952). Mus.
      General considerations of tonality and atonality. Dodecaphony as
      a primarily contrapuntal technique.

21   Schmidt-Garre, Helmut. "Zwölftonmusik—Ende einer Entwicklung,
      nicht Neubeginn," Melos 19:10-13 (Jan 1952). Mus.
      Twelve-tone technique seen as the end point of a development
      rather than as a new approach to music.

22   Vlad, Roman. "Poetica e tecnica della dodecafonia," Rass mus
      22:23-31 (Jan 1952).
      Expanded version in his Modernità e tradizione (see no. 35).
      On the scope of dodecaphony. Current literature on twelve-tone
      theory discussed.

23   Chailley, Jacques. "Malentendus sur le mot 'atonalité' et quelques
      autres," Vie musicale 2:8 (Feb 1952).
      Toward a definition of the terms "atonality," "dodecaphony," and
      others.

See no. 221 (Köhler, Siegfried. "Was ist Zwölftonmusik?" Apr 1952).

24   Thomson, Virgil. "Reflections," Score, no. 6:11-14 (May 1952).
      Reworked from several articles in his The art of judging music.
      New York, Knopf, 1948.
      General evaluation of the twelve-tone system; its contrapuntal
      nature and its attractiveness for composers.

25   Il diapason: rivista di musica contemporanea, v. 3, no. 7/8 (July/Aug
      1952), 38 p. [Twelve-tone issue.]
      "Questo numero è dedicato alle implicazioni ideali e filosofiche
      della poetica dodecafonica."
      Partial contents: Résumés in French and English, p. 5-8; Mila,
      Massimo, "La dodecafonia e la sua offensiva," p. 9-15; Rondi,
      Brunello, "La dodecafonia e il messaggio dell'ordine nello spirito
      contemporaneo," p. 16-18; Kaefer, Johannes, "Essenza della dode-
      cafonia," p. 19-21; Vlad, Roman, "Elementi metafisici nella poetica
      dodecafonia," p. 22-26 (reprinted in his Storia della dodecafonia;
      see no. 116); Magnani, Luigi, "Schönberg e il simbolismo," p. 27-32.

26   Engelmann, Hans Ulrich. "Dodekaphonie und Musikgeschichte," Melos
      19:273-276 (Oct 1952).
      Twelve-tone technique and the philosophy of music history.

See no. 339 (Adorno, Theodor Wiesengrund. "Arnold Schönberg," 1953).

27 Pfrogner, Hermann. Die Zwölfordnung der Töne. Zürich, Amalthea
    [1953]. 280 p.
       Development of the twelve-tone technique not a result of growing
       chromaticism, but of individual psychological concepts, such as
       Schoenberg's idea of the unity of musical space, derived from
       Swedenborg and Balzac.

28 [Keller, Hans]. "First performances and their reviews," Mus rev
    14: 55-59 (Feb 1953). Mus.
       On the audibility of the twelve-tone technique. A diatribe against
       George Perle, Eric Blom, and others. Musical examples from
       Schoenberg's op. 33A and Searle's Shadow of Cain.

29 Goléa, Antoine. Esthétique de la musique contemporaine. Paris,
    Presses universitaires de France, 1954, xix +˙205 p.
       "Ce livre n'est pas une histoire de la musique, mais une consi-
       dération esthétique des principaux courants de la musique con-
       temporaine."
       Partial contents: "Le dodécaphonisme," p. 48-71; Alban Berg, p.
       52-56, 66-71; Pierre Boulez, p. 176-189, 193; John Cage, p. 183-
       184; Luigi Dallapiccola, p. 143-147; René Leibowitz, p. 179-180;
       Bruno Maderna, p. 187; Luigi Nono, p. 186-189; Arnold Schoenberg,
       p. 48-52, 56-63; Humphrey Searle, p. 186; Karlheinz Stockhausen,
       p. 195; Anton Webern, p. 63-66.

30 La musique et ses problèmes contemporains. Paris, Julliard, 1954,
    127 p. (Cahiers de la Compagnie Madeleine Renaud-Jean Louis Bar-
    rault. Année 2, Cah. 3.) Illus., mus.
       Contents: Barrault, Jean Louis, "Pierre Boulez," p. 3-6; Boulez,
       Pierre, ". . . Auprès et au loin," p. 7-24; Fano, Michel, "Pouvoirs
       transmis," p. 38-51; Philippot, Michel, "Musique et acoustique, ou
       à propos de l'art de combiner les sons," p. 52-65; Martenot,
       Maurice, "Lutherie électronique," p. 69-75; Pousseur, Henri,
       "Domaines à venir," p. 76-80; Stockhausen, Karlheinz, "Une ex-
       périence électronique [his Composition 1953, no. 2]," p. 82-93;
       Goléa, Antoine, "Deux portraits: Luigi Nono-Karlheinz Stock-
       hausen," p. 112-114.

31 Burkhard, Willy. "Versuch einer kritischen Auseinandersetzung mit
    der Zwölftontechnik," Schw MZ 94:85-93 (Mar 1954). Mus.
       Audibility of inversion, augmentation, and other contrapuntal de-
       vices in twelve-tone music. Examples from Krenek's Invention
       for flute and clarinet.

32 Turchi, Guido. "Critica, esegesi e dodecafonia," Riv mus ital 56:173-
    180 (Apr/Jun 1954).
       On the multiplicity and nature of critical writings on twelve-tone
       music. Contemporary culture and musical criticism.

33 Krenek, Ernst. "Ein Brief zur Zwölftontechnik," Schw MZ 94:173-174
    (May 1954). Mus.
       A reply to Burkhard's article (see no. 31).

See no. 97 (Pannain, Guido. "Origine e significato," Sept 1954).

34   Pizzetti, Ildebrando. "Internationale Musik?" ZfM 115:513-515 (Sept 1954).
On whether the twelve-tone technique is an international style.

35   Vlad, Roman. Modernità e tradizione nella musica contemporanea. Milano, Einaudi, 1955. Mus.
A collection of essays, mostly derived from earlier articles. Partial contents: "L'ultimo Schönberg," p. 158-173; "Note sulla dodecafonia," p. 174-184; "Elementi metafisici nella poetica schönberghiana," p. 185-196; "Dallapiccola," p. 197-211; "'Il Prigioniero' [di Dallapiccola]," p. 212-216.

36   Adorno, Theodor Wiesengrund. "Das Altern der neuen Musik," Der Monat 7:150-158 (May 1955).
Italian translation, by Giacomo Manzoni: "Invecchiamento della musica nuova," Rass mus 27:1-22 (Mar 1957).
Musical radicalism for its own sake no longer meaningful.

37   Adorno, Theodor Wiesengrund. "Zum Verständnis Schönbergs," Frankfurter Hefte 10:418-429 (Jun 1955).
Schoenberg's development of the twelve-tone technique; its philosophical implications and its importance.

38   Boulez, Pierre. "Einsichten und Aussichten," Melos 22:161-164 (Jun 1955), tr. from the French by Hilde Strobel. Mus.
A discussion of the esthetics of the "pointillist" school.

39   Xénakis, Yannis. "La crise de la musique sérielle," Gravesaner Blätter, Heft 1:2-4 (Jul 1955).
Summaries are in German and English.
Philosophy of "totally controlled" serial music.

40   Keller, Hans. "The audibility of serial technique," Mo mus rec 85:231-234 (Nov 1955).
Serial music must be listened to with a "contrapuntal ear."

41   Keller, Hans. "Dodecaphoneys," Mus rev 16:323-329 (Nov 1955). Mus.
Satirical article on "Twelve-tonesmanship" among the post-Webernites (see no. 44).

42   Myhill, John. "Musical theory and music practice," Journal of aesthetics and art criticism 14:191-200 (Dec 1955).
Atonality, p. 191-194.
Twelve-tone theory does not correspond with twelve-tone practice: cites as an example Krenek's Studies in counterpoint (see no. 209).

43   Rochberg, George. "Tradition and 12-tone music," Mandala [Philadelphia] 1:49-70 ([Dec 1955?]).
Brief bibliography, p. 70.
The relationship of musical form to the twelve-tone technique; the nature of twelve-tone material; hexachordal row techniques of Schoenberg and Webern.

44   Mason, Colin. "Dodecaphoneys: a reply," Mus rev 17:90-94 (Feb 1956).
A reply to Hans Keller (see no. 41).

45   Milner, Anthony. "The vocal element in melody," MT 97:128-131 (Mar 1956). Mus.
The "unvocal" character of melodic lines in some twelve-tone music.

46   Kelterborn, Rudolf. "Stilistisch gegensätzliche Entwicklungen auf der Basis der Zwölftontechnik," Schw MZ 96:162-166 (Apr 1956). Mus.
Rhythmic problems in "pointillist" music; total and relative atonality; electronic music as a consequence of totally controlled serial music.

47   Thilman, Johannes Paul. "Die Kompositionsweise mit zwölf Tönen," Musik und Gesellschaft [E. Berlin] 6:247-251 (Jul 1956) and 6:288-292 (Aug 1956). Mus.
Development of the twelve-tone technique. "Rules" of composition, as codified from Krenek and Jelinek; philosophical implications.

48   Sessions, Roger. "Song and pattern in music today," Score, no. 17:73-84 (Sept 1956).
Consequences of total control in music.

49   Milner, Anthony. "The lunatic fringe combed," MT 97:516-518 (Oct 1956).
Do "extreme" composers think musically? Audibility of serial techniques and effects on the audience.

50   Krenek, Ernst. "Alle spalle dei giovani," Incontri musicali 1:51-54 (Dec 1956).
On the aesthetics of "totally controlled" serial music.
English translation in Electronic music (Die Reihe, 1). (See no. 275.)

See no. 166 (Eimert, Herbert. "Von der Entscheidungsfreiheit des komponisten" in Musikalisches Handwerk [Die Reihe, 3]).

51   Goldbeck, Fred. "Séries et hérésies," Schw MZ 97:4-8 (Jan 1957). Mus.
Discussion, in dialogue form, of the various styles of twelve-note music.

52   Rössler, Ernst Karl. "Zeitgenössische Kirchenmusik und christliche Gemeinde," Musik und Kirche 27:12-22 (Jan/Feb 1957).
The religious music of Webern and Schoenberg is mentioned. Twelve-tone technique in church music. Appended is a brief review of Krenek's Lamentatio Jeremiae Prophetae.

53   Rostand, Claude. "Zwölfton-Manierismus," Melos 24:39-42 (Feb 1957), tr. from the French by Helga Böhme.
On the Post-Webern, experimentalist school.

54   Dansk Musiktidsskrift [København], v. 32, no. 2 (May 1957). Mus., port.
"Dette nummer . . . er hovedsagelig helliget tolvtone- og elektronmusik."
Contents: Thybo, Leif, "Menneske-Maskine," p. 29-30; Krenek, Ernst, "Lydteorier: Betragtninger over electron-musik, p. 31-33 (Chapter 9 of his book, De rebus prius factis); Maegaard, Jan, "Dodekafoni—et resumé," p. 34-37 (mus.); Pade, Else Marie, "Lydprofetier?" p. 38-41 (on electronic music; examples of scores by Messiaen and Stockhausen); Bentzon, Johan, "Musik er mere end musik," p. 42-43; also reviews of some twelve-tone and electronic recordings and scores.

55   Santi, Piero. "Conseguenze e inconseguenze delle 'estreme conse-
     guenze,'" Ricordiana 3:342-345 (Jul 1957).
     On totally controlled serial music.

See no. 170 (Adorno, Theodor Wiesengrund. "Kritieren" in Darmstädter
     Beiträge, 1958, p. 7-16).

See no. 168 (Junge Komponisten, 1958; esp. articles by Metzger and
     Eimert).

56   Melichar, Alois. Musik in der Zwangsjacke: die deutsche Musik
     zwischen Orff und Schönberg. [Wien], Wancura [1958]. 280 p. Mus.
     A lengthy attack on modern music, especially serial music; J. M.
     Hauer and Schoenberg are discussed at some length. The lack of
     a table of contents and an index makes this book difficult to use.
     For a commentary upon and extension of Melichar's viewpoint,
     see Korn, Peter Jena. Apropos Zwangsjacke: eine Analyse der
     Angriffstaktik gegen Alois Melichar. Wien, Wancura, 1959. 33 p.

57   Stadlen, Peter. "Serialism reconsidered," Score, no. 22:12-27 (Feb
     1958). Mus.
     German translation: "Kritik am Seriellen," Musica 13:89-98 (Feb
     1959).
     On the question of the audibility of serial technique. Basic falla-
     cies of twelve-tone premises, such as the equivalence of octave
     transpositions. Performance problems of Webern's Piano varia-
     tions, op. 27. [See nos. 59 (Gerhard), 61 (Sessions), 66 (Stadlen),
     and 69 (Perle).]

58   Castiglione, Niccolò. "Il valore del silenzio e della durata nel lin-
     guaggio musicale contemporaneo," Aut aut [Milano], no. 46:196-202
     (Jul 1958).
     The function of silence and durations in serial music.

59   Gerhard, Roberto. "Apropos Mr. Stadlen," Score, no. 23:50-57 (Jul
     1958). Mus.
     An answer to Stadlen's attacks on serialism; some discussion of
     Webern's Piano variations. [See nos. 57 (Stadlen), 61 (Sessions),
     66 (Stadlen), and 69 (Perle).]

60   Piston, Walter. "More views on serialism," Score, no. 23:46-49
     (July 1958).
     Problems, e.g., that of harmonic rhythm, arising from the dis-
     placement of tonal means of organization by serial means.

61   Sessions, Roger. "To the editor," Score, no. 23:58-64 (July 1958).
     A reply to Peter Stadlen's article (no. 57). [See also nos. 59
     (Gerhard), 66 (Stadlen), and 69 (Perle).]

62   Smith, Robert. "Nichtsmusik," Mus rev 19:222-225 (Aug 1958).
     A satire on pointillism.

63   Porena, Boris. "L'avanguardia musicale di Darmstadt," Rass mus
     28:208-214 (Sept 1958).
     Discusses particularly the works and aesthetics of Cage, Stock-
     hausen, and Nono.

64   Walter, Franz. "A l'écoute des musiciens d'avant-garde," Schw MZ
      98:342-345 (Sept 1958).
          General description of the aesthetics and techniques of the "ex-
          perimental" group: Boulez, Stockhausen, Berio, etc.

65   Lang, Paul Henry. "Editorial," MQ 44:503-510 (Oct 1958).
          An evaluation of dodecaphony at mid-century.

66   Stadlen, Peter. "No real casualties?" Score, no. 24:65-68 (Nov 1958).
          A reply and self-justification. [See nos. 57 (Stadlen), 59 (Gerhard),
          61 (Sessions), and 69 (Perle).]

67   Metzger, Heinz-Klaus. "Gescheiterte Begriffe in Theorie und Kritik
      der Musik" in Berichte/Analysen. Wien, Universal Edition [c1959],
      p. 41-49 (Die Reihe, 5).
          Terminology and (mis)conceptions in critical writings on new
          music.

See no. 775 (Scherchen, Hermann. "Stockhausen und die Zeit," 1959).

68   Middleton, Robert E. "Abt," Mus rev 20:52-55 (Feb 1959). Mus.
          A satire on totally controlled serial music.

69   Perle, George. "Theory and practice in twelve-tone music (Stadlen
      reconsidered)," Score, no. 25:58-64 (Jun 1959).
          Further comments on basic problems of serialism. Corrects
          some errors in previous analyses of Berg's Lulu and Lyric
          Suite, and of Schoenberg's Pierrot. [See nos. 57 (Stadlen), 59
          (Gerhard), 61 (Sessions), and 66 (Stadlen).]

70   Ordini: studi sulla nuova musica [Roma], no. 1 (Jul 1959), 115 p.
      English translations by Robert W. Mann and William Weaver.
          Contents: Adorno, Theodor Wiesengrund, "Musica e tecnica
          oggi"/"Technique, Technology, and music today"; Macchi, Egisto,
          "Produzione e consumo della nuova musica"/"The composer, the
          listener, and the new music"; Guàccero, Domenico, "Problemi di
          sintassi musicale"/"Problems of musical syntax"; Titone, Antonio,
          "Ordine e quadridimensionalità"/"Order and quadridimensionality";
          Evangelisti, Franco, "Verso una composizione elettronica"/"To-
          wards electronic composition"; Masullo, Aldo, "La 'struttura'
          nell'evoluzione dei linguaggi scientifici" (not translated); Letture,
          corrispondenze.

71   Eco, Umberto. "L'opera in movimento e la coscienza dell'epoca,"
      Incontri musicali, no. 3:32-54 (Aug 1959).
          Freedom of choice on the part of the interpreter in such recent
          works as Stockhausen's Klavierstücke XI, Berio's Sequenza per
          flauto solo, and Pousseur's Scambi. Problems of such composi-
          tionally "open" works.

72   Ruwet, Nicolas. "Contraddizioni del linguaggio seriale," Incontri
      musicali, no. 3:55-69 (Aug 1959), tr. by Umberto Eco. Mus.
          Contradictions between theory and practice in post-Webern serial
          music (see no. 73).

73   Pousseur, Henri. "Forma e pratica musicale," Incontri musicali,
      no. 3:70-91 (Aug 1959), tr. by Umberto Eco.
          A reply to Nicolas Ruwet's article (see no. 72).

73a Rochberg, George. "Indeterminacy in the new music," Score, no. 26:
    9-19 (Jan 1960).
       The paradox created by the similarity between "totally controlled"
       serial music and "chance" music.

73b Nono, Luigi. "Gitterstäbe am Himmel der Freiheit," Melos 27:69-75
    (Mar 1950). Port.
       Originally given as a speech at the 1959 Darmstadt Festival. Dis-
       cusses the aesthetic problems raised by "chance" elements in
       music. English translation: "The historical reality of music to-
       day," Score, no. 27:41-45 (Jul 1960).

HISTORY

74 Der blaue Reiter. Hrsg. [Wassily] Kandinsky [und] Franz Marc.
    2. Auflage. München, Piper, 1914. 140 p. Illus., mus.
       One of the chief expressionist manifestos.
       Partial contents: Schoenberg, Arnold, "Das Verhältnis zum Text,"
       p. 27-32; Hartmann, Thomas von, "Über Anarchie in der Musik,"
       p. 43-47; Kulbin, N., "Die freie Musik," p. 69-73; Kandinsky,
       Wassily, "Über die Formfrage," p. 74-102. The appendix contains
       a facsimile of the entire Herzgewächse of Schoenberg; Berg's
       song, op. 2, no. 4; and Webern's song, "Ihr tratet zu dem Herde."

75 Steinhard, Erich. "Bemerkungen zum Expressionismus," Die Musik
    15:49-50 (Oct 1922).
       Brief description of expressionism in music.

See no. 128 (Eimert, Herbert. Atonale Musiklehre, 1924).

76 Schoenberg, Arnold. "Gesinnung oder Erkenntnis?" in 25 Jahre
    neue Musik; Jahrbuch 1926 der Universal-Edition. Wien, Universal
    Edition, 1926, p. 21-30.
       On tonality vs. atonality; summary of harmonic developments,
       1900-1925.

See no. 7 (Sessions, Roger. "Music in crisis," Jan/Feb 1933).

77 Stuckenschmidt, Hans Heinz. "Das Zwölftonsystem," Die neue Rund-
    schau 45:301-311 (Sept 1934).
       Changing concepts of harmony and tonality in Debussy, Reger,
       Strauss, Schoenberg, Berg, Hauer, and Krenek.

78 *Wind, Hans E. Die Endkrise der bürgerlichen Musik und die Rolle
    Arnold Schönbergs. Wien, Krystall-Verlag [1935]. 71 p.

See no. 386 (Hill, Richard S. "Schoenberg's tone-rows and the tonal
    system of the future," Jan 1936).

79 Magni Dufflocq, Enrico. La musica contemporanea. Milano, Società
    editrice libraria, 1937. Mus., port.
       Brief and popularized survey.
       Partial contents: "Politonalismo e atonalismo," p. 48-56; "Arnold

Schönberg," p. 142-147; "Anton von Webern," p. 148-149; "Ernest Krenek," p. 152-153; "Alban Berg," p. 156-157.

80 Fleischer, Herbert. La musica contemporanea. Milano, Hoepli, 1938. ["Tr. di A. Hermet in collaborazione con l'autore."]
    Partial contents: "Schönberg," p. 111-134; "Dallapiccola," p. 218-222; "Anton Webern e Alban Berg," p. 224-229; "Krenek," p. 230-233.
    All are surveys, except the Schoenberg article, which is more detailed; these articles discuss expressionism and the twelve-tone technique.

81 *Hijman, Julius. Nieuwe oostenrijkse musiek (Schönberg, Berg, Webern). Amsterdam, Bigot en van Rossum [1938]. 129 p. Illus., mus.
    "Synchronologie: Schönberg, Alban Berg, andere componisten," p. 130-133; "Discographie," p. 134; "Litteratur," p. 135-136.

See no. 136 (Krenek, Ernst. "New developments of the twelve-tone technique," Feb 1943).

82 Salazar, Adolfo. Music in our time: trends in music since the romantic era. Tr. by Isabel Pope. New York, Norton [c1946]. Mus.
    Partial contents: "The road towards atonality," p. 200-210; "Expressionism," p. 211-220; "Expressionism in the theatre," p. 221-230; "The twelve-tone technique: Berg, Webern, Krenek, Hauer," p. 231-247.
    Discussion of some works with musical examples.

83 Schlee, Alfred. "Vienna since the Anschluss," Mod mus 23:95-99 (Spring 1946).
    Primarily on Hauer and Webern.

84 Leibowitz, René. Schoenberg et son école: l'étape contemporaine du language musical. Paris, Janin, 1947.

    _____. Schoenberg and his school: The contemporary stage of the language of music. Tr. by Dika Newlin. New York, Philosophical Library [c1949]. xxvi + 305 p. Mus.
    Contents: "Prolegomena to contemporary music," p. 1-39; "Arnold Schoenberg," p. 41-134; "Alban Berg," p. 135-186; "Anton Webern," p. 187-255; "The structure of contemporary musical speech," p. 256-290; Bibliography and discography, p. 298-305.
    The first important book on the history of the twelve-tone technique, this work suffers from bias and inadequate analyses, but nevertheless is helpful if used with care.
    Lengthy reviews: Luigi Magnani in Rass mus 18:29-37 (Jan 1948); Milton Babbitt in JAMS 3:57-60 (1950).

See no. 484 (Leibowitz, René. Introduction à la musique de douze sons, 1949. Première partie).

See no. 142 (Eimert, Herbert. Lehrbuch der Zwölftontechnik, 1950).

85 Almeyda, Renato. "Atonalistas brasileños," Revista musicale Chilena 6:37-42 (Autumn 1950). Mus.
    History of twelve-tone music in Brazil.

86   Stuckenschmidt, Hans Heinz. Neue Musik. [Berlin], Suhrkamp Verlag,
     1951, 479 p. Mus. (Zwischen den beiden Kriegen, v. 2.)
        A collection of essays, with an appendix of writings by various
     composers and critics. Has an excellent index; extensive musical
     examples, p. 401-424; list of works of 21 20th-century composers,
     p. 425-434; bibliography, p. 435-437; discography, p. 438-460.
     Partial contents: "Der Radikalismus der Jüngeren," p. 13-38 (music
     in the first decades of the 20th century); "Das Jahrzehnt des Ex-
     periments," p. 64-92 (Stravinsky, Schoenberg, Der blaue Reiter,
     Webern, etc.); "Zwölf-töne-technik," p. 144-163 (broad theoretical
     and historical discussion).

87   Thomson, Virgil. "Atonality today," Etude 69:18-19, 64 (Nov 1951).
     Mus. [Reprinted from his Music right and left. New York, Holt,
     1951.]
        A general article, discussing the international situation in twelve-
     tone composition after Schoenberg's death.

88   Mitchell, Donald. "The emancipation of the dissonance: a selected
     bibliography of the writings of composers, theorists, and critics,"
     Hinrichsen's musical yearbook 7:141-152 (1952).
        Lists of twelve-tone composers and of some of their works, and
     a bibliography of writings on atonality and the twelve-tone tech-
     nique. The bibliographical information varies widely in style and
     coverage; evidently compiled from secondary sources.
        Contents: European composers, p. 142-143; British composers,
     p. 144; "Critics and theorists" (i.e., a bibliography of their writ-
     ings), p. 144-152.

89   Reich, Willi. "Versuch einer Geschichte der Zwölftonmusik" in Alte
     und neue Musik: das Basler Kammerorchester . . . 1926-1951.
     Zürich, Atlantis [1952], p. 106-132.
        Bibliography, p. 131-132
        History and theory: Hauer's twelve-tone technique and system of
     notation; Schoenberg, Berg, Webern, Krenek, and some younger
     composers.

90   Rostand, Claude. La musique française contemporaine. [Paris],
     Presses Universitaires de France, 1952, 126 p. Mus.
        "Les dodécaphonistes," p. 105-120: discusses basic serial technique.
     Pierre Boulez, p. 115-116.

     _____. French music today. Tr. by Henry Marx. New York,
     Merlin Press [1957]. 147 p.
        An abridged translation without musical examples. "The dodeka-
     phonists" [sic], p. 127-141.

91   Mellers, Wilfred. "Recent trends in British music," MQ 38:198-199
     (Apr 1952).
        Short article on British twelve-tone school.

See no. 123 (Seiber, Mátyás. "Composition with twelve notes," Jun 1952).

92   Ackere, Jules van. "Schönberg en de atonale school" in his Muziek
     van onze eeuw, 1900-1950: een inleiding tot de hedendaagse toonkunst.
     Antwerpen, De Sikkel, 1954, p. 163-194. Illus.
        A survey.

See no. 29 (Goléa, Antoine. Esthétique de la musique contemporaine, 1954).

93   Herzfeld, Friedrich. Musica nova: die Tonwelt unseres Jahrhunderts.
     [Berlin], Ullstein [c1954]. 334 p. Illus., mus.
         "Angst . . . Angst . . . Angst" (chapter on the history of the twelve-
     tone technique), p. 51-102: "Arnold Schönbergs Frühwerke; die Luft
     von anderen Planeten; Wendung zur Atonalität; die Angst und das
     Es; das Gesetz der Zwölftontechnik; verschiedene Reihen; der
     schwere Weg zu Arnold Schönberg; von der Macht der Zahl; Anton
     von Webern und Alban Berg."

94   Rognoni, Luigi. Espressionismo e dodecafonia: in appendice scritti
     di Arnold Schönberg, Alban Berg, Wassily Kandinsky. [Torino],
     Einaudi, 1954, 395 p. Mus., port.
         Schoenberg and his school, and their relation to the expressionist
     movement in art and music.
         Appendix 1: writings of Schoenberg, p. 231-274; of Berg, p. 277-
         303; of Kandinsky, p. 307-311.
         Appendix 2, part 1: bibliographies, lists of works, discographies.
             Schoenberg, p. 315-335 (includes previously unpublished articles);
             Berg, p. 336-344; Webern, p. 345-351.
                     part 2: general bibliographies. Expressionism, p. 355-
             363; music, p. 367-384.
         Extensive review by Massimo Mila in Rass mus 24:121-128
         (Apr/Jun 1954).

See no. 153 (Searle, Humphrey. "Twelve note music" in Grove's Diction-
     ary of music and musicians, 1954).

95   Wörner, Karl H. Neue Musik in der Entscheidung. Mainz, Schott
     [1954]. 347 p. Mus., port.
         Partial contents: Bibliography, p. 311-329; "Reihenprinzip," p. 220-
     232 (twelve-tone theory); Alban Berg, p. 90-93; Pierre Boulez,
     p. 147; John Cage, p. 181; Luigi Dallapiccola, p. 153-154; Wolfgang
     Fortner, p. 101-104; Josef Hauer, p. 99; Hanns Jelinek, p. 101;
     Ernst Krenek, p. 99-100; René Leibowitz, p. 147; Luigi Nono, p.
     155; Henri Pousseur, p. 147; Arnold Schoenberg, p. 56-67; Karl-
     heinz Stockhausen, p. 107-108; Anton Webern, p. 94-98.

96   Wörner, Karl H. [and others]. "Expressionismus" in Die Musik in
     Geschichte und Gegenwart. Kassel, Bärenreiter, 1954, v. 3, col.
     1655-1675. Mus.
         A history of musical expressionism. Bibliography, col. 1762-1763.

97   Pannain, Guido. "Origine e significato della musica dodecafonica,"
     Nuova antologia [Roma] 462:79-86 (Sept 1954).
         A brief history of the development of the classical twelve-tone
     technique.

98   Myers, Rollo H. "Music in France in the post-war decade," RMA
     Proc 81:93-106 (1954/55).
         The twelve-tone group, p. 97-100; electronic music, p. 102-104.

99   Neighbor, Oliver. "The evolution of twelve-note music," RMA Proc
     81:49-61 (1954/55).
         Concise and clearly written presentation of the history of the

twelve-tone technique: early dodecaphonic procedures in Hauer
and Schoenberg; quasi-serial treatment in Bartók, Debussy,
Stravinsky, and Scriabine; mention of the Russian twelve-tone
composer, Lev Golyshev.

99a Chase, Gilbert. "Twelve-tone composers" in his America's music,
from the Pilgrims to the present. New York, McGraw-Hill [c1955],
p. 597-616.
     Brief discussion of Schoenberg's and Krenek's American works,
     and of the compositions of Stefan Wolpe, Adolph Weiss, Walling-
     ford Riegger, Kurt Liszt, George Perle, Milton Babbitt, Ben
     Weber, and other American serial composers.

100 Collaer, Paul. La musique moderne, 1905-1955. Paris, Elsevier,
1955, iv + 304 p. Mus., port.
     "134 exemples musicaux sous plaquette séparée."
     Partial contents: "Arnold Schoenberg, Anton Webern, Alban Berg,
     expressionisme, atonalité, dodécaphonisme," p. 35-77; John Cage,
     p. 287; Luigi Dallapiccola, p. 272-274; Ernst Krenek, p. 238; Bruno
     Maderna, p. 277; Karlheinz Stockhausen, p. 289.

101 Wiedman, Robert William. Expressionism in music; an interpreta-
tion and analysis of the expressionistic style in modern music.
[Ann Arbor, Mich., University Microfilms], 1955, 487 p. (University
microfilms, no. 12,248.) (Thesis, Ph. D., education, New York University.)
     Not seen; abstract in Dissertation Abstracts 15:1189-1190 (Jul
     1955).

102 Carsalade du Pont, Henri de. "La musique dodécaphoniste," Etudes
[Paris], no. 287:363-365 (Dec 1955).
     A history of the development of the twelve-tone school and of
     its most important composers.

103 Gottschalk, Nathan. Twelve note music as developed by Arnold
Schoenberg, with an analysis of two representative works for violin.
68 l. Mus. (Thesis, D. M. A., Boston University, 1956.)
     Partial contents: "The dissolution of the modal and tonal sys-
     tems," p. 7-13; "The twelve note music of Schoenberg," p. 14-25;
     "Analysis of Tripartita of Richard Hoffmann," p. 26-32; "Analysis
     of Phantasy for violin with piano accompaniment, op. 47, by
     Arnold Schoenberg," p. 33-40; "Performance of contemporary
     music," p. 41-42; appendices (tone-row analyses); bibliography,
     p. 67-68.
     The historical résumé seems to be patterned largely after Lei-
     bowitz (see no. 84); the analyses are primarily row and thematic
     analyses. Useful but somewhat superficial.

104 Smith Brindle, Reginald. "The origins of Italian dodecaphony," MT
97:75-76 (Feb 1956).
     A brief history of the adoption of the twelve-tone technique in
     Italy.

105 Hartog, Howard, ed. European music in the twentieth century.
London, Routledge and Kegan Paul [1957]. viii + 341 p.
     Partial contents: Goehr, Walter, and Goehr, Alexander, "Arnold

Schoenberg's development towards the twelve-note system," p. 76-93; Hamilton, Iain, "Alban Berg and Anton Webern," p. 94-117; White, Eric Walter, "Stravinsky" (twelve-tone works), p. 54 et passim; Milner, Anthony, "English contemporary music" (Roberto Gerhard, p. 146; Mátyás Seiber, p. 146; Humphrey Searle, p. 146-147); Smith Brindle, Reginald, "Italian contemporary music" (Luigi Dallapiccola, p. 176-181; Bruno Maderna, p. 184, 185-186; Luigi Nono, p. 184, 186-187); Hartog, Howard, "German contemporary music" (Wolfgang Fortner, p. 197); Drew, David, "Modern French music" (Pierre Boulez, p. 292-294).

See no. 496 (Redlich, Hans Ferdinand. "The second Viennese school," in his Alban Berg, 1957, p. 13-18).

106 Pestalozza, Luigi. "I compositori milanesi del dopoguerra," Rass mus 27:27-43 (Mar 1957).
The younger Milanese composers, including Luciano Berio and Bruno Maderna. Short biographical sketches, p. 41-43.

107 Stuckenschmidt, Hans Heinz. "German musical life: patterns of conservatism and experiment," Atlantic monthly 199:167-171 (Mar 1957).
The German twelve-tone school, p. 170-171. A very general article.

108 Searle, Humphrey. "A new kind of music," Twentieth century [London] 161:480-483 (May 1957).
The post-Webern composers; a brief summary.

See no. 614 (Hodier, Andre. "The young French music," May 25, 1957).

109 Rostand, Claude. "L'Italie musicale actuelle," Table ronde, no. 117:79 (Sept 1957).
A very brief survey of Italian contemporary music, especially the serial composers: Dallapiccola, Peragallo, Maderna, Vlad, Nono, Berio, Prosperi, and others.

110 Schatz, Hilmar. "Theoretiker des Zufalls: junge Komponisten dozieren bei den Darmstädter Ferienkursen," Melos 24:298-300 (Oct 1957). Port. [of Luigi Nono].
One of the better of the many articles written about the Darmstadt Summer School; clearly summarizes the general activities there and the trend of the post-Webern composers who participate.

111 Gradenwitz, Peter. "Reihenkomposition im Orient" in Bericht über den Internationalen Musikwissenschaftlichen Kongress, Wien; Mozartjahr 1956. Hrsg. von Erich Schenk. Graz, Hermann Böhlaus, 1958, p. 238-241.
A brief résumé of twelve-tone activities in the Middle and Far East, especially in Israel and Japan.

See no. 786 (Kirchmeyer, Helmut. Igor Strawinsky, 1958).

112 Prieberg, Fred K. Lexikon der neuen Musik. Freiberg, Karl Alber, 1958, x + 495 p. Illus., mus.
Entries related to serial music include: Hans Erich Apostel,

p. 10-11; Atonalität, p. 13-16; Henk Badings, p. 21-22; Alban Berg,
p. 36-41; Luciano Berio, p. 42; Pierre Boulez, p. 53-55; John Cage,
p. 67-68; Luigi Dallapiccola, p. 87-90; Hanns Eisler, p. 110-112;
Elektronische Musik, p. 116-121; Hans Ulrich Engelmann, p. 122;
Wolfgang Fortner, p. 139-142; Jef Golyschew [Lev Golyshev], p.
167; Josef Matthias Hauer, p. 185; Hans Werner Henze, p. 187-
189; Hanns Jelinek, p. 221-222; Giselher Klebe, p. 228-229; Ernst
Krenek, p. 234-238; René Leibowitz, p. 254-255; Elizabeth Lutyens,
p. 262-263; Bruno Maderna, p. 263; Jan Maegaard, p. 263; Riccardo
Malipiero, p. 268; Riccardo Nielsen, p. 318; Luigi Nono, p. 318-
320; Mario Peragallo, p. 331-332; Henri Pousseur, p. 344-345;
Wallingford Riegger, p. 365-366; Giacento Scelsi, p. 376; Arnold
Schoenberg, p. 381-392; Humphrey Searle, p. 398-399; Mátyás
Seiber, p. 399-401; Igor Strawinsky, p. 405-416; Camillo Togni,
p. 429; Roman Vlad, p. 440; Anton Webern, p. 446-449; Zwölftonmusik, p. 458-462.

113   Searle, Humphrey. "Atonal and serial music" in Simpson, Robert
Wilfred, ed. Guide to modern music on records (1958). [London],
Anthony Blond [c1958], p. 151-172.
A general discussion of twelve-tone composers and of the re-
cordings to date of twelve-tone and electronic music. List of
records, p. 170-172.

114   Simbriger, Heinrich. "Die heutige Situation der Zwölftonmusik" in
Bericht über den Internationalen Musikwissenschaftlichen Kongress,
Wien; Mozartjahr 1956. Hrsg. von Erich Schenk. Graz, Hermann
Böhlaus, 1958, p. 593-598.
Post-Schoenbergian concepts of serial technique.

115   Stuckenschmidt, Hans Heinz. Schöpfer der neuen Musik: Portraits
und Studien. [Frankfort am Main], Suhrkamp Verlag, 1958. 301 p.
Biographical and stylistic discussions.
Partial contents: "Igor Strawinsky," p. 128-161; "Stil und Asthetik
Schönbergs," p. 162-179 (from Schw MZ, Mar 1958; see no. 306);
"Alban Berg," p. 180-191; "Anton von Webern," p. 192-203; "Luigi
Dallapiccola," p. 228-240; "Hans Werner Henze," p. 290-301.

116   Vlad, Roman. Storia della dodecafonia. Milano, Suvini Zerboni
[1958]. 395 p. Mus.
The most comprehensive history of the twelve-tone technique
published to date; broad but rather superficial.
Contents: "Acquisizione dello spazio dei dodici suoni," p. 13-21;
"Premesse dei nuovi principi strutturali," p. 23-32; "Applicazioni
parziali del metodo dodecafonico," p. 45-58; "Prime musiche do-
decafoniche per orchestra," p. 59-70; "Prime opere teatrali dode-
cafoniche," p. 71-84; "Aspetti metafisici della poetica dodecafonica," p. 85-94; "Ricupero di elementi tradizionali nell'ultimo peri-
odo creativo di Schönberg," p. 95-114; "Berg e la libera articolazione della dodecafonia," p. 115-124; "I traguardi del radicalismo di Webern," p. 125-130; "Diffusione della dodecafonia," p. 131-
160; "Strawinsky e la dodecafonia," p. 161-174; "Influsso della
dodecafonia su compositori che non ne adottano integralmente il
metodo," p. 175-192; "La dodecafonia in Italia," p. 193-254; "La

serialità integrale e la musica elettronica," p. 255-274; "Luigi
Dallapiccola," p. 275-314; "Le opere postume di Schönberg,"
p. 315-328; "'Agon' di Strawinsky," p. 329-338.

See no. 393 (Wellesz, Egon. The origins of Schönberg's twelve-tone
   system; 1958).

117   Henderson, Robert L. "Schönberg and 'expressionism,'" Mus rev
      19:125-129 (May 1958).
      Discussion of the literature on Schoenberg and the Viennese
      school; thesis is that most writings ignore the social and cul-
      tural background of Vienna at the turn of the century.

118   Stuckenschmidt, Hans Heinz. "Sitten und Gebräuche der Neutöner,"
      Der Monat 11:51-57 (Dec 1958).
      A history of the I.S.C.M. and a discussion of the younger gen-
      eration of composers.

See no. 306a (Adorno, Theodor Wiesengrund. "Zur Vorgeschichte der
   Reihenkomposition" in his Klangfiguren, 1959, p. 95-120).

See no. 174 (Cage, John. "Zur Geschichte der experimentellen Musik in
   der Vereinigten Staaten" in Darmstädter Beiträge, v. 2, 1959).

See no. 174 (Wörner, Karl H. "Neue Musik 1946-1958: Versuch eines
   historischen Uberblicks" in Darmstädter Beiträge, v. 2, 1959).

118a Zillig, Winfried. Variationen über neue Musik. [München], Nym-
      phenburger Verlagshandlung [c1959]. 283 p. Illus.
      Partial contents: "Die Antipoden: Arnold Schönberg und Igor
      Strawinsky," p. 11-12; "Strawinsky und das Zwölftonsystem," p.
      50-59; "Schönberg und sein Weg von der Tonalität zum Zwölf-
      tonsystem," p. 61-107; "Alban Berg und die Wiener Schule," p.
      140-148; "Die Erneuerung der italienischen Musik von Malipiero
      bis Dallapiccola," p. 165-173; "Anton Webern, Aussenseiter und
      Vorbild," p. 181-190; "Die Jungen: Stockhausen, Boulez, Nono,
      Berio," p. 190-199; "Krenek, der Sucher," p. 236-239; "Neue
      Musik in Deutschland: Pepping, Genzmer, Fortner, Henze, Klebe,"
      p. 254-263; "Zusammenfassung und Ausblick," p. 263-270; Litera-
      turverzeichnis, p. 283.

118b Perle, George. "Atonality and the twelve-note system in the United
      States," Score, no. 27:51-66 (Jul 1960). Mus.
      An historical survey.

ANALYSIS AND THEORY

COMPOSITIONAL TECHNIQUES

Introductory Articles Addressed to the Layman

119   Costarelli, Nicola. "Nota sulla dodecafonia," Rass mus 15:267-271
      (Sept/Oct 1942). Mus.
      A simple article on the principles of the twelve-tone technique.

120 Carner, Mosco. "Technique of twelve-note music," The Listener
41:1040 (June 16, 1949).
A general and brief description of the use of the row.

121 Symkins, L. O. "Arnold Schoenberg's new world of dodecaphonic
music," Etude 68:12-14 (Sept 1950). Illus., mus.
Includes a very brief description of the row treatment in Schoenberg's piano piece, op. 33a.

See no. 325 (Salazar, Adolfo. "Arnold Schoenberg post-mortem," 1951).

122 Rostand, Claude. "Dodécaphonisme," Larousse mensuel 12:712-713
(Sept 1951). Mus.
A simple explanation.

123 Seiber, Mátyás. "Composing with twelve notes," Mus sur 4:472-489
(Jun 1952). Mus.
". . . script . . . originally prepared for a 30-minutes' broad-
cast."
A clear and excellent article for the layman. Examples from
Schoenberg's 3rd and 4th Quartets, Berg's Violin Concerto,
Webern's Three songs, op. 23, and other works.

See no. 301 (Rostand, Claude. "Note sommaire sur le système dodécaphonique et la méthode sérielle" in Stuckenschmidt, Hans Heinz,
Arnold Schoenberg, 1956, p. 139-143).

124 Fiebig, Kurt. "Was ist Zwölftonmusik?" Der Kirchenchor [Kassel]
16:66-69 (Sept/Oct 1956). Mus.
Somewhat more penetrating than most introductory articles.

125 Cecchi, César. "Qué es la dodecafonía," Revista musical Chilena
11:8-15 (Apr/May 1957).
Elementary article on the theory of dodecaphony.

Technical and Specialized Works

126 *Hauer, Josef Matthias. Vom Wesen des Musikalischen: ein Lehrbuch der atonalen Musik. Berlin, Schlesinger [c1923]. 61 p. Diagrs.,
mus.
An enlarged edition of his Über die Klangfarben, 1919.

127 Hauer, Josef Matthias. "Atonale Musik," Die Musik 16:103-106
(Nov 1923).
Elaborate system of comparison of tonal and atonal music. Per-
mutations of the arrangement of the twelve tones.

128 Eimert, Herbert. Atonale Musiklehre. Leipzig, Breitkopf und
Härtel, 1924, iv + 36 p. Mus., tables.
Part 1: theory and practice; atonality and the twelve-tone tech-
nique (melody, harmony, form, etc.).
Part 2: historical and aesthetic discussions.
One chapter from this book was published as "Zum Kapitel:
atonale Musik," Die Musik 16:899-904 (Sept 1924).
A comment on this chapter, by Josef Matthias Hauer: "Offener
Brief [an Herbert Eimert]," Die Musik 17:157 (Nov 1924).

129   Hauer, Josef Matthias. Von Melos zur Pauke: eine Einführung in
       die Zwölftonmusik. Wien, Universal Edition [1925]. 21 p. (His
       Theoretische Schriften, Bd. 1.) Mus., tables.
          A little manual of twelve-tone technique, with brief discussions
       of harmony, melody, rhythm, etc. Tables of tropes.

130   *Hauer, Josef Matthias. Zwölftontechnik, die Lehre von den Tropen.
       Wien, New York, Universal Edition [1926]. xii + 23 p. (His Theore-
       tische Schriften, Bd. 2.) Mus.

131   Mersmann, Hans. Die Tonsprache der neuen Musik. Mainz, Melos-
       verlag/Schotts Söhne [c1928]. Mus.
          On theoretical problems of 20th-century music. Examples drawn
       from Schoenberg, Krenek, Berg, Webern.

See no. 6 (Reich, Willi. "Grenzgebiete der neuen Töne," Nov 1932).

See no. 10 (Krenek, Ernst. Über neue Musik, 1937).

See no. 295 (Weiss, Adolph. "The twelve-tone series" in Armitage, Merle
       (ed.), Schoenberg, 1937, p. 75-77).

132   Nathan, Hans. "The Viennese Lied, 1910-37," Modern music 14:136-
       142 (Mar/Apr 1937). Mus.
          Technique of song composition, from Mahler to Schoenberg,
       Berg, Webern, and Hauer. Melody, rhythm, accompaniment,
       relation of text and music.

133   Slonimsky, Nicolas. "The plurality of melodic and harmonic sys-
       tems," PAMS 3:16-24 (1938). Mus.
          "Twelve-tone system," p. 17-24.
          Principle of nonrepetition of tones; division of the row into hexa-
       chords.

134   Perle, George. "Evolution of the tone row: the twelve-tone modal
       system," Mus rev 2:273-287 (Nov 1941). Mus., tables.
          The nonmotivic function of the row: its modal application.

135   Krenek, Ernst. "Cadential formations in twelve-tone music," BAMS,
       no. 6:5 (Aug 1942).
          An abstract only.
          The modality concept of the row; three cadential types.

136   Krenek, Ernst. "New developments of the twelve-tone technique,"
       Mus rev 4:81-97 (Feb 1943). Mus.
          Secondary series derivations; hexachords; modality.

137   Eschman, Karl. Changing forms in modern music. Boston, E. C.
       Schirmer [c1945]. xii + 180 p. Mus.
          The twelve-tone systems of Hauer and Schoenberg, p. 83-110.
          Discusses the changes that have occured in the 20th century in
       musical aesthetics and in the elements of music (phrase struc-
       ture, harmony, variation technique, etc.).

138   Babbitt, Milton. The function of set structure in the twelve-tone
       system. [Unpublished MS. Princeton, N. J. ? 1946.]
          Not seen. Undoubtedly highly technical. (Reference taken from
       Perle, no. 196.)

139 *Jachino, Carlo. Tecnica dodecafonica, trattato pratico. Milano,
     Curci [1948]. 19 p. Mus.

See no. 13 (Adorno, Theodor Wiesengrund. Philosophie der neuen Musik,
     1949).

140 Heiss, Hermann. Elemente der musikalischen Komposition (Tonbe-
     wegungslehre). Heidelberg, Hochstein [1949]. 207 p. Mus.
       Most of the musical examples seem to be from the author's
       own compositions.
       Partial contents: "Der Zwölftonsatz," p. 145-205: "Abstrakte
       Darstellung," p. 145-153; "Die kompositorische Handhabung," p.
       154-173; "Die Trope," p. 174-180; "Das Kontinuum (Formbildung),"
       p. 181-205.

See no. 484 (Leibowitz, René. Introduction à la musique de douze sons,
     1949. Première partie).

141 Le système dodécaphonique. Paris, Richard-Masse [1949]. 83 p.
     Mus. (Polyphonie, cahier 4.)
       Contents: "Résolution du premier Congrés international pour la
       musique dodécaphonique," p. 5-6; Schoenberg, Arnold, "La compo-
       sition à douze sons," tr. by René Leibowitz, p. 7-31; Leibowitz,
       René, "Aspects récents de la technique de douze sons," p. 32-53;
       Saby, Bernard, "Un aspect des problèmes de la thématique séri-
       elle," p. 54-63; Krenek, Ernst, "Technique de douze sons et classi-
       cisme," p. 64-67; Martin, Frank, "Schoenberg et nous," p. 68-71;
       Dallapiccola, Luigi, "A propos d'un trait 'expressionniste' de
       Mozart," p. 72-79; "Un musicien d'aujourd'hui: ené Leibowitz,"
       p. 80-83 (portrait and list of works).
       Review by Milton Babbitt in JAMS 3:264-267 (Fall 1950); pri-
       marily a discussion of Schoenberg's article, "La composition à
       douze sons" (see no. 143).

142 Eimert, Herbert. Lehrbuch der Zwölftontechnik. Wiesbaden, Breit-
     kopf und Härtel, 1950, 61 p. Mus., tables.

     *_____. 2. verm. Aufl. 1952. 64 p.

     *_____. 3. Aufl. 1954 [c1952]. 64 p.

     *_____. Manuale di tecnica dodecafonica. Prefazione e note di
     Luigi Rognoni. [Tr. di Mariangela Donà.] Milano, Carisch, 1954,
     84 p.
       Part 1: Theory of the twelve-tone technique, including intervallic
       inversions; tonal elements in twelve-tone music; row systems
       (e.g., all-interval rows); statistics.
       Part 2: Form in twelve-tone music.
       Part 3: History of the twelve-tone technique (see nos. 17, 19).

143 Schoenberg, Arnold. "Composition with twelve tones" in his Style
     and idea. New York, Philosophical Library [c1950], p. 102-143. Mus.
       "Delivered as a lecture at U. C. L. A., March 26, 1941."
       Schoenberg's exposition of his development and use of the twelve-
       tone technique. Use of the four forms of the row; manipulation
       of the basic set in composition.
       French translation, as "La composition à douze sons," in no. 141.

Important reviews: Dean, Winton, "Schoenberg's ideas," M & L 31:295-304 (Oct 1950); Babbitt, Milton (see no. 141).

144   Brainard, Paul. A study of the twelve-tone technique. (Thesis, M. A., University of Rochester, 1951.) 74 l., mus.
Contents: Atonality and the development of the row; general characteristics; technique of the row; [Berg's] Lyric Suite; functions of the tone row; bibliography.

145   Chailley, Jacques. Traité historique d'analyse musicale. Paris, A. Leduc [1951]. v + 130 p. Mus.
"La musique atonale," p. 77-87 (includes serial music).
Definition of atonal and serial music; examples of "classical" serial techniques from Schoenberg and Webern.

See no. 86 (Stuckenschmidt, Hans Heinz. "Zwölf-töne-technik" in his Neue Musik, 1951, p. 144-163).

See no. 89 (Reich, Willi. "Versuch einer Geschichte der Zwölftonmusik," 1952).

146   Boulez, Pierre. "Eventuellement," Rev mus, no. 212:117-148 (Apr 1952). Diagrs., mus.
Technical article on serial organization of rhythm and other non-pitch elements. Future of "totally controlled" serial music.

See no. 392 (Perle, George. "Schönberg's late style," Nov 1952).

147   *Bentzon, Niels Viggo. Tolvtoneteknik. København, W. Hansen, 1953. 82 p. Illus.
Review in Nordisk Musikkultur 4:129-130 (Dec 1953).

148   [omitted]

149   Malipiero, Riccardo. "La dodecafonia come tecnica," Riv mus ital 55:277-300 (Jul/Sept 1953). Mus.
Questions discussed at the Primo Congresso per la Musica Dodecafonica, Milano, 1949.
Rather general article, dealing with tonality, atonality, and the characteristics of dodecaphony.

150   Krenek, Ernst. "Is the twelve-tone technique on the decline?" MQ 29:513-527 (Oct 1953). Mus.
A discussion of post-Schoenbergian dodecaphony; the use of hexa-chords, row permutation and rotation; "totally organized" serial music.

See no. 93 (Herzfeld, Friedrich. Musica nova, 1954).

151   Rufer, Josef. Composition with twelve notes related only to one another. Tr. by Humphrey Searle. London, Rockliff [c1954]. xiv + 218 p. Mus. (24 p. of musical examples inserted between p. 214-215.)
Appendix 1: "Contemporary composers on their experiences of composition with twelve notes": Boris Blacher, p. 177-178; Luigi Dallapiccola, p. 178-181; Wolfgang Fortner, p. 181-183; Roberto Gerhard, p. 183-185; Hans Werner Henze, p. 185; Richard Hoff-

mann, p. 185-186; Hanns Jelinek, p. 186-188; Ernst Krenek, p. 188-191; Rolf Liebermann, p. 191-193; Humphrey Searle, p. 193-195; Mátyás Seiber, p. 196-198; Rudolf Wagner-Régeny, p. 198-200; Winfried Zillig, p. 200-201.
Appendix 2: "Arnold Schoenberg: sketch for a series of lectures [on composition]," p. 202-204; "Complete list of Arnold Schoenberg's musical and literary works," p. 205-214.
A textbook of twelve-tone composition, with Schoenberg as a model. Important review by Richard S. Hill in Notes 12:223-225 (Mar 1955).

152   Schoenberg, Arnold. "Apollonian evaluation of a Dionysian epoch" in his Structural functions of harmony. London, Williams and Norgate [1954], p. 192-196.
      Brief description of the method of composing with twelve tones, and criticism of some compositional procedures in contemporary music.

153   Searle, Humphrey. "Twelve-note music" in Grove's Dictionary of music and musicians. 5th ed. London, Macmillan, 1954, v. 8:617-623. Mus.
      Includes a short bibliography. Some examples of Hauer's system of notation.

See no. 95 (Wörner, Karl H. Neue Musik in der Entscheidung, 1954).

154   Erickson, Robert. The structure of music: a listener's guide; a study of music in terms of melody and counterpoint. New York, Noonday Press, 1955. xi + 208 p. Mus.
      Many examples drawn from Schoenberg, Berg, and Webern.

155   Ogdon, Wilbur Lee. Series and structure: an investigation into the purpose of the twelve-note row in selected works of Schoenberg, Webern, Kronek and Leibowitz. [Ann Arbor, Mich., University Microfilms], 1955. 341 p., mus. (University microfilms, no. 14,663.) (Thesis, Ph. D., Indiana University.)
      Primarily a row analysis of Schoenberg's Op. 33a, Webern's Variations for piano, Krenek's Symphonic elegy, Leibowitz's Third Quartet, and other works by these composers.

156   Rochberg, George. The hexachord and its relation to the twelve-tone row. Bryn Mawr, Pa., Presser [c1955]. viii + 40 p. Mus., tables.
      A manual on symmetrical row construction: hexachords related by mirror inversion; interchangeable hexachords.
      Important reviews by Richard S. Hill in Notes 12:223-225 (Mar 1955) and by George Perle in JAMS 10:55-59 (Spring 1957) [Discusses "combinatoriality"].

157   Babbitt, Milton. "Some aspects of twelve-tone composition," Score 12:53-61 (Jun 1955). Mus.
      Highly technical and important article, on his theory of combinatoriality and on music totally controlled by serial principles. Discusses developments in the U. S.

158   Keller, Hans. "Strict serial technique in classical music," Tempo [ser. 2], no. 37:12-24 (Autumn 1955). Mus.

"The present essay . . . proposes to demonstrate that two great 18th-century composers [Beethoven and Mozart] did in fact [use] the method of composing with tone rows."

159   Ballif, Claude. Introduction à la métatonalité: vers une solution tonale et polymodale du problème atonal. Paris, Richard-Masse [c1956]. 116 p. Tables. (Polyphonie, cahier 11/12.)
       "Tonalité et atonalité," a comparison of tonal and atonal melody, counterpoint, harmony, and form, p. 69-76; "Tonal analysis" of Schoenberg's Piano piece, op. 19, no. 25, p. 111.

See no. 103 (Gottschalk, Nathan. Twelve-note music as developed by Arnold Schoenberg, 1956).

160   Perle, George. Serial composition and atonality. [Ann Arbor, Mich. University Microfilms], 1956 [c1959]. 211 p. Mus. (Thesis, Ph. D., New York University, Graduate school of arts and sciences.)
       Contents: "Tonality, atonality, dodecaphony," p. 1-12; "'Free' atonality," p. 13-48; "Non-dodecaphonic serial composition," p. 49-79; "Motivic functions of the set," p. 80-110; "Simultaneity," p. 111-160; "Structural functions of the set," p. 161-199; Index to basic definitions, p. 200; Bibliography, p. 201-211.
       Includes a discussion of the technical procedures employed in the nonserial and atonal and in the twelve-tone compositions of Schoenberg, Berg, and Webern, and a description of non-dodeca-phonic serial procedures in some of the works of Debussy, Scriabine, Roslavetz, Bartók, Stravinsky, and in Schoenberg's op. 23 and 24.

161   Smith Brindle, Reginald. "The lunatic fringe: III, computational composition," MT 97:354-356 (Jul 1956). Mus.
       Serial organization of rhythmic and other non-tone elements; examples from Dallapiccola, Donatoni, Togni, and Maderna.

See no. 47 (Thilman, Johannes Paul. "Die Kompositionsweise mit zwölf Tönen," Jul 1956; Aug 1956).

162   Milhaud, Darius. "Konstruierte Musik," Gravesaner Blätter, Heft 5:14-15 (Aug 1956). Musical examples, p. 9-13.
       A brief description of Milhaud's experience with the technique of total control.

163   Gerhard, Roberto. "Developments in twelve-tone technique," Score, no. 17:61-72 (Sept 1956).
       Gerhard's use of the twelve-tone technique. Combinatoriality; derivation of rhythmic series from tone row.

164   Simbriger, Heinrich. "Die Situation der Zwölftonmusik," Musik und Kirche 26:209-223 (Sept/Oct 1956). Mus.
       An explanation of Hauer's and Schoenberg's twelve-tone principles; the twelve-tone technique in church music.

165   Dallin, Leon. Techniques of twentieth century composition. Dubuque, Iowa, W. C. Brown [c1957]. xix + 223 p. Mus.
       "The twelve-tone technique," p. 180-194.
       A textbook which summarizes the techniques of contemporary

composition. Examples in this chapter are taken from Schoenberg and Krenek; Webern is relegated, along with the post-
Webern composers, to a chapter on "special effects."

166   Musikalisches Handwerk. Wien, Universal Edition [c1957]. 88 p.
Diagrs., mus. (Die Reihe: Information über serielle Musik, 3.)

Musical craftmanship. Bryn Mawr, Pa., Theodore Presser [c1959].
88 p. Diagrs., mus. (Die Reihe: a periodical devoted to developments in contemporary music, 3.)
      Contents of American edition: Eimert, Herbert, "The composer's
      freedom of choice," tr. by Leo Black, p. 1-9; Stockhausen, Karl-
      heinz, ". . . how time passes . . .," tr. by Cornelius Cardew,
      p. 10-40; Cage, John, "To describe the process of composition
      used in 'Music for piano 21-52,'" p. 41-43; Pousseur, Henri,
      "Outline of a method: introduction [p. 44-47], Quintet in memory
      of Webern [p. 48-55], Impromptu [p. 56-63], Variations I [p. 64-
      81], Variations II [p. 82-88]," tr. by Leo Black.

See no. 496 (Redlich, Hans Ferdinand. "The problem of tonality" in his
Alban Berg, 1957, p. 19-31).

166a Rufer, Josef. "Was ist Zwölftonmusik?" NZfM 118:11-13 (Jan 1957);
118:552-553 (Oct 1957); and 119:14-16 (Jan 1958). Mus.
      The first two articles deal with the technique in general; the
      third shows its treatment in Schoenberg's Fourth Quartet.

See no. 110 (Schatz, Hilmar. "Theoretiker des Zufalls," Oct 1957).

167   Kelterborn, Rudolf. "Gegensätzliche Formprinzipien in der zeitgenössischen Musik," Schw MZ 97:472-474 (Dec 1957).
      Permutational principle in serial music.

168   Junge Komponisten. Wien, Universal Edition [c1958]. 133 p. Diagrs.,
mus., tables. (Die Reihe: Information über serielle Musik, 4.)
      Contents: Lewinsky, Wolf-Eberhard von, "Junge Komponisten,"
      p. 5-8; Unger, Udo, "Luigi Nono," p. 9-17; Koenig, Gottfried
      Michael, "Henri Pousseur," p. 18-31; Stephan, Rudolf, "Hans
      Werner Henze," p. 32-37; Ligeti, György, "Pierre Boulez," p. 38-
      63; Metzger, Heinz-Klaus, "Intermezzo I: das Alten der Philoso-
      phie der neuen Musik," p. 64-80; [Eimert, Herbert], "Intermezzo
      II: Adorno und Kotschenreuther," p. 81-83; Koenig, Gottfried
      Michael, "Bo Nilsson," p. 85-88; Lewinsky, Wolf-Eberhard von,
      "Giselher Klebe," p. 89-97; Santi, Piero, "Luciano Berio," p. 98-
      102; Schubert, Reinhold, "Bernd Alois Zimmermann," p. 103-112;
      Manzoni, Giacomo, "Bruno Maderna," p. 113-118; Schnebel, Die-
      ter, "Karlheinz Stockhausen," p. 119-133.

169   Reti, Rudolf Richard. Tonality, atonality, pantonality: a study of
some trends in twentieth century music. London, Rockliff [c1958].
xii + 166 p. Mus.
      Part two, atonality: Schoenberg's search for a new style, p. 33-
      41; Composition with twelve tones, p. 42-48; Twelve-tone tech-
      nique in evolution, p. 49-55.

170   Steinecke, Wolfgang, ed. Darmstädter Beiträge zur neuen Musik.
[V. 1.] Mainz, Schott [c1958]. 100 p. Diagrs., mus., ports.

Contents: Schoenberg, Arnold [a brief untitled article from his unpublished writings], p. 5-6; Adorno, Theodor Wiesengrund, "Kritieren," p. 7-16; Krenek, Ernst, "Bericht über Versuche in total determinierter Musik," p. 17-21; Fortner, Wolfgang, "Kranichsteiner Aspekte," p. 22-24; Nono, Luigi, "Die Entwicklung der Reihentechnik," tr. by Willi Reich, p. 25-37 (technical article, with analyses of row treatment in the theme of Schoenberg's Variations for Orchestra, op. 31, in Webern's Variations for Orchestra, op. 30, and in Boulez' Structures; Stockhausen's Komposition Nr. 2 für Sinustöne, and Zeitmasse are also discussed; describes and illustrated the technique of row permutation); Pousseur, Henri, "Webern und die Theorie," p. 38-43; Boulez, Pierre, "Alea," tr. by Heinz-Klaus Metzger, p. 44-56 [Italian tr. in Incontri musicali, no. 3:3-15 (Aug 1959); discusses function of chance in composition]; Stockhausen, Karlheinz, "Sprache und Musik," p. 57-81 (detailed discussion of the vocal and serial techniques in Boulez's Le marteau sans maître, Nono's Il canto sospeso, and Stockhausen's Gesang der Jünglinge); Henze, Hans Werner, "Wo stehen wir Heute?" p. 82-83; Kolisch, Rudolf, "Über die Krise der Streicher," p. 84-90; Stuckenschmidt, Hans Heinz, "Entwicklung oder Experiment?" p. 91-93; "Zwölf Jahre Kranichstein, Chronik 1946-1958," p. 94-100.

170a Stephan, Rudolf. Neue Musik: Versuch einer kritischen Einführung. Göttingen, Vandenhoeck & Ruprecht [c1958]. 74 p. Mus.
    The compositional techniques of Schoenberg, Berg, Webern, and Stockhausen are discussed on p. 36-67.

171 Payne, Elsie. "The theme and variation in modern music," Mus rev 19:112-124 (May 1958). Mus.
    Variation technique in serial music, p. 115-117; examples from Schoenberg and Webern.

172 Krenek, Ernst. "Was ist Reihenmusik?" NZfM 119:278-281 (May 1958) and 119:428-430 (Aug 1958).
    The concepts of serialism and the twelve-tone technique; the serialization of non-pitch elements. An answer to questions raised by Rufer (see no. 166).

173 Kagel, Mauricio. "Ton-Cluster, Anschäge, Übergänge" in Berichte/Analysen. Wien, Universal Edition [c1959], p. 23-37. Diagrs. (Die Reihe: Information über serielle Musik, 5.)
    Tone clusters and similar procedures as compositional resources used in serial composition.

174 Steinecke, Wolfgang, ed. Darmstädter Beiträge zur neuen Musik. v. 2. Mainz, Schott [c1959]. 94 p.
    Contents: Wörner, Karl H., "Neue Musik 1946-1958: Versuch eines historischen Überblicks," p. 7-14; Pousseur, Henri, "Theorie und Praxis in der neuesten Musik," p. 15-29; Stockhausen, Karlheinz, "Musik im Raum," p. 30-35 (see no. 772); Berio, Luciano, "Musik und Dichtung: eine Erfahrung," p. 36-45 (see no. 609); Cage, John, "Zur Geschichte der experimentellen Musik in den Vereinigten Staaten," p. 46-53; Metzger, Heinz Klaus, "Hommage

à Edgard Varèse," p. 54-66; Nono, Luigi, "Vorword zum Kranich-steiner Kompositions-Studio 1958," p. 67-68; "Kranichsteiner Chronik, 1958," p. 69-74; "Neue Musik in Darmstadt 1946-1958," p. 75-94.

175   Clarke, Henry Leland. "The abuse of the semitone in twelve-tone music," MQ 45:295-301 (Jul 1959).
      Tonal implications of the half-step. Suggests use of all-interval rows and other solutions.

*175a Spinner, Leopold. A short introduction to the technique of twelve-tone composition. New York, Boosey & Hawkes, 1960. 37 p. Mus.

175b Babbitt, Milton. "Twelve-tone invariants as compositional determi-nants," MQ [special issue on the Princeton Seminar in Advanced Musical Studies] 46:246-259 (Apr 1960). Diagrs.
      Technical article on set structure.

See no. 739a (Krenek, Ernst. "Extents and limits of serial techniques," Apr 1960).

175c Walker, Alan. "Back to Schönberg," Mus rev 21:140-147 (May 1960). Mus.
      Audibility of serial derivations, as determined by experiments with listeners.

HARMONY

176   Alaleona, Domenico. "I moderni orizzonti della tecnica musicale; teoria della divisione dell'ottava in parti ugali," Riv mus ital 18: 382-420 ([Apr/Jun] 1911). Mus.
      Pre-twelve-tone theories on the harmonic implications of the equal division of the octave into twelve parts. Purely theoretical article.

177   Alaleona, Domenico. "L'armonia modernissima: le tonalità neutre e l'arte di stupore," Riv mus ital 18:769-838 ([Oct/Dec] 1911). Mus.
      Chromatic tonal harmony at the point of its change to atonality; a theory of musical expressionism. An important and little-known article.

178   Hauer, Josef Matthias. "Die Tropen und ihre Spannungen zum Drei-klang," Die Musik 17:257-258 (Jan 1925). Mus.
      Resolutions of six-note chords (tropes) to triads.

179   Klein, Fritz Heinrich. "Die Grenze der Halbtonwelt," Die Musik 17:281-286 (Jan 1925). Mus., tables.
      On atonal harmony: number of possible chords, etc.

180   Pisk, Paul. "The tonal era draws to a close," Modern music 3:3-7 (Mar/Apr 1926).
      A summary of Hauer's and Schoenberg's new harmonic principles.

181   Erpf, Hermann Robert. Studien zur Harmonie- und Klangtechnik der neueren Musik. Leipzig, Breitkopf und Härtel, 1927. 235 p. Mus.

General discussion of twelve-tone music, p. 83-86; examples from works of Schoenberg.

182 Hábá, Alois. Neue Harmonielehre des diatonischen, chromatischen, viertel-, drittel-, sechstel- und zwölftel-Tonsystems. Leipzig, Kistner & Siegel, 1927. xviii + 251 p. Mus., tables.
No index; difficult to use. A manual of all the possible chord combinations and scale patterns in each of these harmonic systems.

183 Deutsch, Leonhard. "Das Problem der Atonalität und des Zwölftonprinzip," Melos 6:108-118 (Mar 1927).
"Tries to prove that all possible combinations of the twelve tones may be referred back to altered diatonic chords, therefore the twelve-tone system as such . . . has no justification" (Richard Hill, "Schoenberg's tone-rows and the tonal system of the future," p. 16-17). (See no. 386.)

184 Schoenberg, Arnold. "Problems of harmony," Modern music 11:167-187 (May/Jun 1934). Tr. by Adolph Weiss. Mus.
"First presented as a lecture during Mr. Schoenberg's recent professorship at the Berlin Akademie der Künste." Also appears in Armitage, ed., Schoenberg. 1937 (see no. 295).
Weakening of tonality by means of chromaticism; twelve-tone technique as another means of organizing music; new concepts of dissonance (see no. 192).

See no. 77 (Stuckenschmidt, Hans Heinz. "Das Zwölftonsystem," Sept 1934).

185 Schoenberg, Arnold. "Tonality and form," Pacific Coast musician [Los Angeles] 24:3 (May 4, 1935).
A refutation of the concept that musical form is impossible without tonality.

186 Taylor, Noel Heath. "The Schoenberg concept," M & L 20:183-188 (Apr 1939).
Schoenberg's theory of harmony.

187 Kessler, Hubert. "Some problems of tonality in relation to Schönberg's twelve-tone technique," JAMS 1:49-50 (Fall 1948).
Abstract only.
Does the twelve-tone technique exclude tonality? "Laws" of twelve-tone music related to those of tonal music.

188 *Brauner, Rudolph Franz. Vom Dreiklang zum Zwölftonakkord: ein Rückblick auf die Entwicklung des Tonsatzes von Bach bis Hindemith. Wien, Verlag für Jugend und Volk, 1949. 284 p. Mus., diagr.

189 Jelinek, Hanns. "Versuch über der Sinn der Verwendung von Zwölftonreihen," Melos 18:252-255 (Sept 1951). Port.
Harmonic problems and overtone bases of the twelve-tone technique.

190 Jelinek, Hanns. Anleitung zur Zwölftonkomposition nebst allerlei Paralipomena. Appendix zu [Jelineks] "Zwölftonwerk," op. 15. Erster Teil: Allgemeiner und vertikale Dodekaphonik. Wien, Universal Edition, c1952. 106 p. Mus.

_____. Anhang zu Anleitung zur Zwölftonkomposition. Tabellen und Kompositionsbeispiele von Schoenberg, Webern und Jelinek. [Wien] Universal Edition [1952]. Unpaged. Mus.

> A manual of composition. This first part deals only with harmony; a second part treats of counterpoint (see no. 215); and a future third part is to cover "broken" dodecaphony. Almost all the examples are from the author's composition, "Zwölftonwerk." [See Roland Tenschert's article, "Hanns Jelinek: zu seinem 'Zwölftonwerk,' op. 15" (no. 715).]
>
> An important review by Ernst Krenek is in MQ 40:250-256 (Apr 1954). (See no. 712.)

191 Gerhard, Roberto. "Tonality in twelve-tone music," Score, no. 6:23-35 (May 1952). Mus.

> The twelve-note technique as a new principle of tonality. "Classical" row treatment and permutational treatment. Possible chords in dodecaphonic harmony.

192 Yasser, Joseph. "A letter from Arnold Schoenberg," JAMS 6:53-62 (Spring 1953). Mus.

> A reply from Schoenberg to a letter from Yasser on Schoenberg's article in Modern music (see no. 184). Twelve-tone technique and problems of equal temperament; consonance and dissonance; small and large intervals.

193 Costère, Edmond. "Entre l'harmonie classique et les harmonies contemporaines, y a-t-il rupture, ou continuité?" Revue de musicologie 36:55-65 (Jul 1954). Mus.

> "Nous examinerons successivement l'incidence des relations cardinales: 1° sur l'accord dit de septième de dominante; 2° sur l'échelonnement diatonique; 3° sur un example de musique dite primitive; 4° sur un exemple de musique sérielle; 5° sur un exemple de musique contemporaine par superpositions de sons fixes."

194 Perle, George. "The possible chords in twelve-tone music," Score, no. 9:54-58 (Sept 1954). Tables.

> The number of different chord combinations possible in twelve-tone music. Corrects figures in Gerhard's article (see no. 191).

195 Gerhard, Roberto. "Reply to George Perle," Score, no. 9:59-60 (Sept 1954). Mus.

> Further corrections of errors in chord tables in Gerhard's article of May, 1952 (see nos. 191, 194).

196 Perle, George. "The harmonic problem in twelve-tone music," Mus rev 15:257-267 (Nov 1954). Mus.

> How the row governs the vertical ordering of sound. Discusses Babbitt's theory of combinatoriality (see no. 157).

197 *Neumann, Friedrich. Tonalität und Atonalität: Versuch einer Klärung. Landsberg a. Lech, H. Hohler, 1955. 30 p. Mus. (Beiträge zu Gegenwartsfragen der Musik, 1.)

198 Keller, Hans. "Serial octave transpositions," Mo mus rec 86:139-143 (Jul/Aug 1956); and 86:172-177 (Sept/Nov 1956). Mus.

Problems created by the identity of complementary intervals in
"classical" twelve-tone music.

199   Gould, Glenn. "The dodecaphonist's dilemma," Canadian music
journal 1:20-29 (Autumn 1956). Mus.
Harmonic problems of the post-Webern composers; division of
the row into hexachords and three-note groups.

200   Forneberg, Erich. Der Geist der neuen Musik: der neue Klang im
Spiegel der traditionellen Harmonielehre. Würzburg, Triltsch, 1957,
xxvi + 130 p.; Anhang [mus. and illus.] 42 p. (Literar-historisch-
musikwissenschaftliche Abhandlungen, 15.)
Contents: bibliography, p. xviii-xxvi; "Der Geist der neuen Musik,"
p. 22-78; "Das 'Neue' in der zeitgenössischen Musik," p. 79-113
("Die Komposition mit zwölf Tönen," p. 98-113).

201   Prosperi, Carlo. L'atonalità nella musica contemporanea. Caltanis-
setta [Sicily], S. Sciascia [1957]. 47 p. Mus. (Lo Smeraldo, 7.)
A brief general discussion.

202   Frid, Géza. "Twaalf contra twaalf," Mens en melodie 12:366-369
(Dec 1957). Mus.
The author suggests another twelve-tone "system" (originated by
a theorist named Ernö Landvai), based on functional tonal rela-
tions (see no. 203).

203   "Twaalf contra twaalf; standpunten inzake de dodecafonie," Mens en
melodie 13:16-19 (Jan 1958).
Articles by Hendrik Andriessen, Géza Frid, and Harry Mayer;
further commentary on Frid's article (see no. 202).

204   Truscott, Harold. "The real atonalism," Chesterian 33:35-44 (Autumn
1958).
"Atonality" only an extreme form of chromatic tonality; tonality
"normal" but atonality "abnormal."

204a   Rochberg, George. "The harmonic tendency of the hexachord,"
Journal of music theory 3:208-230 (Nov 1959). Mus.
Serial structure based on symmetrically arranged hexachords
produces a new type of harmonic order. Discusses Hauer's
tropes and Babbitt's source sets. Hexachordal analysis of
Schoenberg's op. 45 and 50b.

MELODY

205   Stuckenschmidt, Hans Heinz. "Vocal style in the twentieth century,"
Modern music 13:3-13 (Mar 1936). Mus.
Schoenberg, Krenek, and Berg, p. 5-8; a brief discussion, not a
melodic analysis.

See no. 388 (Jalowetz, Heinrich. "On the spontaneity of Schoenberg's
music," Oct 1944).

See no. 141 (Saby, Bernard. "Un aspect des problèmes de la thématique
serielle" in Le système dodécaphonique, 1949).

206   Johnson, Martha. A study of linear design in Gregorian chant and music written in the twelve-tone technique. Minneapolis, Burgess, 1954, p. 69-99. Mus. (Hamline studies in musicology, ed. by Ernst Krenek, v. 1.)
       Melodic analyses of Webern's String quartet, op. 28, Schoenberg's Fourth string quartet, and Krenek's Lamentatio Jeremiae.

207   Scriabine, Marina. "Athématisme et fonction thématique dans la musique contemporaine" in Inventaire des techniques rédactionnelles. Paris, Richard-Masse [1954], p. 35-46. (Polyphonie, 9ᵉ/10ᵉ cahier.)
       Résumé of the last chapters of a "work in preparation," Les perspectives de la musique contemporaine.
       So-called athematicism as an "ultra-thematicism"; the characteristics of themes.

See no. 154 (Erickson, Robert. The structure of music, 1955).

See no. 45 (Milner, Anthony. "The vocal element in melody," Mar 1956).

See no. 351 (Skrebkow, S. "Gegen die Atonalität Schönbergs," May 1957).

See no. 215 (Jelinke, Hanns. Anleitung zur Zwölftonkomposition. Zweiter Teil, 1958).

RHYTHM

208   Boulez, Pierre. "Propositions" in Le rythme musical. Paris, Richard-Masse [1948], p. 65-72. Mus. (Polyphonie, 2ᵉ cahier.)
       Rhythmic treatment in Stravinsky and Boulez.

See no. 146 (Boulez, Pierre. "Eventuellement," Apr 1952).

See no. 618 (Barraqué, Jean. "Rythme et développement," 1954).

See no. 157 (Babbitt, Milton. "Some aspects of twelve-tone composition," Jun 1955).

See no. 46 (Kelterborn, Rudolf. "Stilistisch gegensätzliche Entwicklungen auf der Basis der Zwölftontechnik," Apr 1956).

See no. 599 (Elston, Arnold. "Some rhythmic practices in contemporary music," Jul 1956).

See no. 161 (Smith Brindle, Reginald. "The lunatic fringe, III," Jul 1956).

See no. 163 (Gerhard, Roberto. "Developments in twelve-tone technique," Sept 1956).

See no. 58 (Castiglione, Niccolò. "Il valore del silenzio e della durata," Jul 1958).

See no. 166 (Stockhausen, Karlheinz. ". . . How time passes . . ." in Musical craftsmanship, 1959, p. 10-40).
       Detailed and technical analysis of his serial treatment of rhythmic elements; the relation of pitches to frequencies, and frequencies to tempi.

COUNTERPOINT

209   Krenek, Ernst. Studies in counterpoint based on the twelve-tone technique. New York, Schirmer [c1940]. ix + 37 p. Mus.

————. Zwölfton-Kontrapunkt-Studien. Tr. by Heinz Klaus Metzger. Mainz, Schott, 1952, 51 p. Mus.
    Textbook of the twelve-tone technique approached through counterpoint (see no. 42).

210   Thilman, Johannes Paul. Problems der neuen Polyphonie. Dresden, Dresdener Verlagsgesellschaft [1949 ?]. 111 p.
    Contains much discussion of twelve-tone music. No music examples; no analyses; no index.
    Contents: "Einleitung," p. 7-18; "Melodik," p. 19-37; "Harmonik," p. 38-55; "Polyphonie," p. 56-75; "Form," p. 76-87; "Rhythmus," p. 88-98; "Klangverwirklichung," p. 99-102; "Sinn," p. 103-109.

See no. 20 (Hall, Richard. "Twelve-tone music and tradition," 1952).

See no. 24 (Thomson, Virgil. "Reflections," May 1952).

211   Searle, Humphrey. Twentieth century counterpoint. London, Williams and Norgate [1954]. ix + 158 p. Mus.
    Partial contents: "The development of chromatic counterpoint," p. 7-21; "Schoenberg and twelve-note composition," p. 71-117; "Postscript" (includes some comments on recent twelve-tone composers), p. 47-150.

See no. 31 (Burkhard, Willy. "Versuch einer kritischen Auseinandersetzung mit der Zwölftontechnik," Mar 1954).

See no. 154 (Erickson, Robert. The structure of music, 1955).

212   Herzfeld, Friedrich. "Der Reiz des Krebses: Bedeutungswandel einer Kompositionsform," NZfM 11:71-74 (Nov 1955). Mus.
    On the contrapuntal device of retrograde motion; some discussion of its use in serial music.

See no. 40 (Keller, Hans. "The audibility of serial technique," Nov 1955).

213   Unger, Udo. Die Klavierfuge im zwanzigsten Jahrhundert. Regensburg, Gustav Bosse, 1956. 147 p. Mus., tables. (Kölner Beiträge zur Musikforschung, 11.)
    Partial contents: "Fuge und Zwölftontechnik," p. 107; "Fuge und serielle Technik," p. 108; "Analyse von W[olfgang] Fortners Fuge aus 'Kammermusik,' komp. 1943," p. 91-92.

214   Adorno, Theodor Wiesengrund. Die Funktion des Kontrapunkts in der neuen Musik. [Berlin-Dahlem, Akademie der Künste, 1958]. [43 p.] (Anmerkungen zur Zeit, 4.)
    Counterpoint in contemporary music, especially in the twelve-tone school.

215   Jelinek, Hanns. Anleitung zur Zwölftonkomposition nebst allerlei Paralipomena; Appendix zu "Zwölftonwerk," op. 15. Zweiter Teil: Horizontal Dodekaphonik, Kombination und Abteilungen. Wien, Universal Edition [1958]. 107-239 p. + [110 p.] Mus.

Not seen; entry from M.L.A. <u>Notes</u> 16:576 (Sept 1959).
(See no. 190.)

216   [omitted]

NOTATION

217   Wirtz, Warren. "The problem of notation in the twelve-tone technique," <u>Mus rev</u> 7:103-110 (May 1946). Mus.
A new notational system.

218   Schnippering, H. "Atonalität und temperierte Stimmung," <u>Melos</u>
17:9-11 (Jan 1950). Mus.
On the notation of atonal music.

219   Gindele, Father Corbinian. "Von cis nach c," <u>Melos</u> 17:169 (Jun
1950). Mus.
A reply to Schnippering (see no. 218).

220   Schnippering, H. "Von der Logik der Zwölftonmusik," <u>Melos</u> 17:312-
314 (Nov 1950). Mus.
On the notation of atonal music, III (see nos. 218 and 219).

<u>See no. 89</u> (Reich, Willi. "Versuch einer Geschichte der Zwölftonmusik"
<u>in</u> Alte und neue Musik, 1952).

221   Köhler, Siegfried. "Was ist Zwölftonmusik? Eine kritische Wertung,"
<u>Musica</u> 6:142-144 (Apr 1952). Mus.
Definition of twelve-note music; discussion of the problem of
notation.

<u>See no. 153</u> (Searle, Humphrey. "Twelve-note music" <u>in</u> Grove's Diction-
ary of music and musicians, 1954).

<u>See no. 238</u> (Meyer-Eppler, Werner. "Elektronische Musik," Dec 6, 1954).

<u>See no. 279</u> (Prieberg, Fred. "Erste elektronische Partitur," Apr 1957).

<u>See no. 263</u> ("The progress of science," Jan 1958).

II
ELECTRONIC MUSIC

PHILOSOPHY AND CRITICISM

222 Beyer, Robert. "Die Klangwelt der elektronischen Musik," ZfM 113:74-79 (Feb 1952). Illus.
Composition of "Klangfarbenmusik"; implications of electronic music.

See no. 30 (La musique et ses problèmes contemporains, 1954).

223 Beyer, Robert. "Elektronische Musik," Melos 21:35-39 (Feb 1954).
Electronic music as a development of Klangfarbenmelodie; its problems and implications.

224 Beyer, Robert. "Zur Situation der elektronischen Musik," ZfM 116:452-456 (Aug/Sept 1955).
Electronic music as the beginning of a new era in music. Its relation to the serial music of Schoenberg and Webern. Klangfarbenmelodie.

225 Suder, Alexander L. "Die überflüssige Windmaschine; eine Betrachtung zur 'Elektronischen Musik,'" ZfM 116:456-459 (Aug/Sept 1955).
Fallacies of the assumptions and philosophy of electronic music.

226 Keller, Wilhelm. "Elektronische Musik und musique concrète," Merkur [Stuttgart] 9:877-881 (Sept 1955).
A definition and description of each; aesthetic implications.

227 Dahlhaus, Carl, and Stephan, Rudolf. "Eine 'dritte Epoche' der Musik? Kritische Bemerkungen zur elektronische Musik," Dt Univ Zt 10:14-17 (Sept 12, 1955).
Philosophical considerations; discussion of problems raised in Elektronische Musik (Technische Hausmitteilungen des Nordwestdeutscher Rundfunk, 1954) and Elektronische Musik (Die Reihe, 1). (For the latter, see no. 275.)

228 Rognoni, Luigi. "La musica 'elettronica' e il problema della tecnica," Aut aut, no. 36:450-461 (Nov 1956).
Drawn from two lectures given at Darmstadt in July 1956: "Musik der jungen Generation: Kompositions und Interpretations-Probleme" and "Die Frage der Technik in der elektronischen Musik."

See no. 54 (Dansk Musiktidsskrift, May 1957).

229 Metzger, Heinz-Klaus. "Nochmals 'Wider die Natur'; zur Frage der Verwendung der menschlichen Stimme in elektronischer Musik,"

NZfM 118:329-330 (May 1957).
On the use of voices in electronic music.

230   Berio, Luciano. "Sur la musique electronique," Schw MZ 97:265
(Jun 1957).
Brief statement written for the I.S.C.M. festival in Zürich,
June, 1957.

See no. 257 (Stuckenschmidt, Hans Heinz. "Il mondo delle sonorità ignote,"
Jul 1957).

231   Pfrogner, Hermann. "Elektronik—Lust am Untergang?" NZfM
118:484-489 (Sept 1957). Illus.
Busoni's and Schoenberg's thoughts on new means of musical
production; Klangfarbenmelodie. Attacks electronic music.

See no. 260 (Prieberg, Fred K. "Musik: Töne aus der Elektronröhre,"
Nov 1957).

See no. 261 (Becerra, Gustavo. " ¿Que es la música electrónica?" Dec
1957).

See no. 275 (Stuckenschmidt, Hans Heinz. "The third stage" in Electronic
music, 1958, p. 11-13).

232   Babbitt, Milton. "Who cares if you listen?" High fidelity 8:38-40,
126-127 (Feb 1958).
A plea for research in experimental electronic music. The
author feels that "advanced music" should be intended primarily
for specialists.

233   Boulez, Pierre. "Son, verbe, synthèse," Melos 25:310-313 (Oct 1958).
[German tr. by Hilde Strobel, p. 313-317.] Illus.
Fusion of sound and word by electronic means, and resulting
expansion of sound possibilities.

See no. 70 (Evangelisti, Franco. "Verso una composizione elettronica"/
"Towards electronic composition" in Ordini, Jul 1959).

DESCRIPTION AND HISTORY

See no. 611 (Scriabine, Marina. "Pierre Boulez et la musique concrète,"
1952).

234   Eimert, Herbert. "Was ist elektronische Musik?" Melos 20:1-5
(Jan 1953). Illus.
A brief history and description. (For English translation see
no. 275.)

235   Beyer, Robert. "Zur Geschichte der elektronischen Musik," Melos
20:278-280 (Oct 1953).
Brief history of electronic music; includes bibliographical notes.

236   Eimert, Herbert. "Möglichkeiten und Grenzen der Elektronischen
Musik," Schw MZ 93:445-447 (Nov 1953).

Definition of electronic music; differences from musique concrète. Brief history and summary of objectives.

237 Eimert, Herbert. "Elektronische Musik" in Die Musik in Geschichte und Gegenwart. Kassel, Bärenreiter, 1954, v. 3, col. 1263-1267. Illus. Includes "nontechnical" bibliography. (For French translation, see no. 253.)

See no. 95 (Wörner, Karl H. "Die Klangwelt der elektronischen Musik" in his Neue Musik in der Entscheidung, 1954, p. 296-302).
History and description of electronic music, especially as developed at the Cologne Studio.

238 Meyer-Eppler, Werner. "Elektronische Musik: Gestaltungsmöglichkeiten, Notation, Technische Einrichtungen," Dt Univ Zt 9:9-10 (Dec 6, 1954). Diagr.
Description of technical considerations.

See no. 98 (Myers, Rollo H. "Music in France in the post-war decade," 1954/55).

239 Gravesano: Musik, Raumgestaltung, Elektroakustik. Hrsg. von Dr. [Werner] Meyer-Eppler. Mainz, Ars Viva [c1955]. 140 p. Diagrs., illus., mus.
A collection of articles, primarily devoted to technical considerations of acoustics and of electronic instruments. Some brief bibliographies.

240 *Klangstruktur der Musik. Neue Erkenntnisse musik-elektronischer Forschung: Vortragsreihe "Musik und Technik" des Ausseninstitutes der Technischen Universität Berlin-Charlottenburg, mit Vorträgen von B[oris] Blacher [et al.] ergänzt durch Beiträge von F. Enkel [et al.]. Im Auftrage des Ausseninstitutes der Technischen Universität zusammengestellt und bearb. von F[ritz] Winckel. Berlin, Verlag für Radio-Foto-Kinotechnik [1955].
Reviewed in Dansk Musiktidsskrift 32:49 (May 1957).

241 "News and comments. Italy. Electronic music," Score, no. 11:67 (Mar 1955).
Very brief résumé of activities at the Milan Studio.

242 Koster, Ernst. "Kinderkrankheiten der elektrogenen Musik," Musica 9:315-317 (Jul 1955). Mus.
Brief description of "experimentelle elektrogene Musik"; explanation of basic terms (sine tone, overtone, timbre, frequency, etc.).

243 Sonner, Rudolf. "Elektronische Musik; ihre drei Arbeitsberichte," ZfM 116:449-452 (Aug/Sept 1955).
Brief history of the development of electronic instruments and of electronic music.

244 Krenek, Ernst. "New development in electronic music," Musical America 75:8 (Sept 1955).
Simple, nontechnical description for the layman.

245 Vlad, Roman. "Die Reihe and electronic music," Score, no. 13:23-24 (Sept 1955).
Current status of electronic music; brief history.

246   Berio, Luciano. "Prospettive nella musica: richerche ed attività
       dello Studio di Fonologia Musicale di Radio Milano," Elettronica
       5:108-115 (1956).
           History of the activities at the Milan Studio.

247   *Prieberg, Fred K. Musik im Technischen Zeitalters. Zürich,
       Atlantis [1956]. 176 p. Mus.
           Bibliography, p. 173-176.

248   Oesch, Hans. "Einführung in die elektronische Musik," Universitas
       [Stuttgart] 11:167-175 (Feb 1956).
           The development of electronic music is discussed. Brief bibliog-
           raphy, p. 175.

249   Smith Brindle, Reginald. "The lunatic fringe: I. Electronic music,"
       MT 97:200-201 (Jun 1956).
           A brief historical summary.

250   Pestalozza, Luigi. "L'ultima avanguardia: post-Weberniani, concerti
       ed elettronici," Ricordiana [nuova serie] 2:333-336 (Jul 1956).
           Brief history and description of the European musical avant-garde
           (Boulez, Schaeffer, et al.).

251   Forte, Allen. "Composing with electrons in Cologne," High fidelity
       6:64-67, 156, 159 (Oct 1956). Illus.
           Nontechnical article, discussing the activities at the Cologne
           Studios. Describes equipment, discusses composers, defines
           terminology.

252   Stockhausen, Karlheinz. "A proposito di musica elettronica," Incon-
       tri musicali, no. 1:70-78 (Dec 1956).
           Nontechnical; description of electronic music and discussion of
           its aesthetic problems.

253   Vers une musique expérimentale. Sous la direction de Pierre
       Schaeffer. Paris, Richard-Masse [1957]. xvi + 141 p. Mus., diagrs.
       (La revue musicale, no. 236.)
           Partial contents: Schaeffer, Pierre, "Vers une musique expéri-
           mentale," p. 11-27; Boulez, Pierre, "Tendances de la musique
           récente," p. 28-35 (on the music of Varése, Messiaen, Stock-
           hausen, Cage); Goléa, Antoine, "Tendances de la musique con-
           crète," p. 36-44; Eimert, Herbert, "Musique électronique," tr. by
           Charles Hebert, p. 45-49 (a translation of his article in M. G. G.;
           see no. 237); Ussachevsky, Vladimir, "La 'tape music' aux États-
           Unis," p. 50-55; Scherchen, Hermann, "Depassement de l'orches-
           tre," p. 56-59; Tardieu, Jean, "Décade de musique expérimentale,"
           p. 103-104; Poullin, Jacques, "Son et espace," p. 105-114; Moles,
           André, "Machines à musique," p. 115-127; Arthuys, Philippe, "La
           pensée et l'instrument," p. 128-134; "Le group de recherches de
           musique concrète," p. 135-136; "Historique de la musique con-
           crète," p. 137-138; "List des oeuvres de musique concrète," p.
           139-141.

254   Tall, Joel. "Music without musicians," Saturday review 40:56-57
       (Jan 26, 1957).
           Brief history and description of electronic music, musique con-
           crète, and "music for tape recorder."

255   Maren, Roger. "Electronic music: untouched by human hands,"
       Reporter 16:40-42 (Apr 18, 1957).
       A summary of the activities in Europe and the U.S. in the
       fields of electronic music and musique concrète.

256   "Das neue Buch: elektronische Musik in Italien," Melos 24:139-140
       (May 1957).
       On the activities of the Studio di Fonologia Musicale in Milan;
       review of the periodicals Elettronica and Incontri musicali, and
       a description of electronic music.

257   Stuckenschmidt, Hans Heinz. "Il mondo delle sonorità ignote: Un
       contributo all'estetica della musica elettronica," Aut aut, no. 41:399-
       406 (Jul 1957).
       Historical and aesthetical summary.

258   Nettel, Reginald. "Electronic music," Mo mus rec 87:163-168
       (Sept/Oct 1957).
       Brief summary of the current status of electronic music.

259   Berio, Luciano. "Note sulla musica elettronica," Ricordiana [nuova
       serie] 3:427-437 (Oct 1957).
       Comparatively nontechnical article.

260   Prieberg, Fred K. "Musik: Töne aus der Elektronröhre," Monat
       10:62-66 (Nov 1957).
       A brief history of mechanical music (from the 1920's) and of
       electronic music; aesthetic problems are discussed.

261   Becerra, Gustavo. "¿Que es la música electrónica?" Revista musi-
       cale chilena 11:27-44 (Dec 1957). Diagrs.
       Contents: "Las conjeturas usuales," p. 27-28; "Algunos aspectos
       fundamentales," p. 28-38; "Actuales compromisos estilísticos de
       la música electrónica," p. 38-40; "Proyecciones artísticas de la
       música electrónica," p. 40-42; "Sus efectos económicos y soci-
       ales," p. 42-43; "Conclusiones," p. 43-44.

262   Manzoni, Giacomo. "Breve introduzione alla musica elettronica,"
       Rass mus 27:309-315 (Dec 1957).
       Explanation of the instruments used; the activities at the studios
       at Cologne, Paris, and Milan. Mentions some composers and
       their works. Nontechnical article.

See no. 112 (Prieberg, Fred K. "Elektronische Musik" in his Lexikon der
       neuen Musik, 1958, p. 116-121).

See no. 116 (Vlad, Roman. "La serialità integrale e la musica elettronica"
       in his Storia della dodecafonia, 1958).

263   "The progress of science: electronic music," Discovery 19:4-5 (Jan
       1958). Illus.
       A concise and clear summary of the apparatus and technique
       used and of the objectives of electronic music. Illustrates the
       "Darmstadt method of notation for electronic music."

264   Smith Brindle, Reginald. "Reports from abroad: Italy, the R.A.I.
       Studio di Fonologia Musicale at Milan," MT 99:98 (Feb 1958).

Very brief article commenting on the broadcasts of electronic
music given by Luciano Berio. Discusses the use and implications of non-tone sounds derived from "white noise."

265   Prieberg, Fred K. "Italiens elektronische Musik," Melos 6:194-198
(Jun 1958). Illus.
Activity of the Studio di Fonologia Musicale in Milan.

266   Badings, Henk. "Electronic music: its development in the Netherlands," Delta: a review of arts, life and thought in the Netherlands,
1:85-93 (Winter 1958/59). Illus., mus.
A nontechnical history of Dutch electronic music.

See no. 770 (Luening, Otto. "Karlheinz Stockhausen," Winter 1958/59).

267   Experiences musicales: musiques concrète, electronique, exotique,
par le Groupe de recherches musicales de la Radiodiffusion Télé-
vision française. Paris, Richard-Masse [c1959]. 72 p. Mus., diagrs.
(La revue musicale, no. 244.)
        Contents: Messiaen, Olivier, "Préface"; Ferrari, Luc, "Les
        étapes de la vision"; Schaeffer, Pierre, "Situation actuelle de la
        musique expérimentale"; Mâche, François-Bernard, "Connais-
        sance des structures sonores"; Xénakis, Yannis, "Notes sur un
        'Geste électronique'"; Boucourechliev, André, "La fin et les mo-
        yens"; Philippot, Michel, "Espace vital"; Vandella, Romuald,
        "Musique exotique et musique expérimentale"; Poullin, Jacques,
        "L'orielle et le malentendu"; Moles, Abraham A., "Instrumenta-
        tion électronique et musiques expérimentales"; Schaeffer, Pierre,
        "Le Groupe de recherches musicales . . ."; Chambure, Alaine
        de, "Infrastructure technique"; Ferrari, Luc, "Les étapes de la
        production"; "Historiques des recherches de musique concrète";
        "Bibliographie sommaire"; "Discographie"; "Notices biographiques"
        (on Berio, Boucourechliev, Pousseur, Maderna, and other elec-
        tronic and concrète composers).

268   Hiller, Lejaren Arthur. "Experimental music" in Experimental
music: composition with an electronic computer, by Lejaren A.
Hiller, Jr., and Leonard M. Isaacson. New York, McGraw-Hill,
1959, p. 36-57, 124-131.
        Definition of various types of experimental music: electronic
        music, musique concrète, tape-recorder music, computational
        and computer music. Numerous bibliographical footnotes.

268a Rondi, Brunello. Il cammino della musica d'oggi e l'esperienza
elettronica. Padova, Rebellato, 1959. 113 p.
        Not seen; bibliographical information from the Bibliografia
        Nazionale Italiana, 1959:V.

269   Stockhausen, Karlheinz. "Elektronische und instrumentale Musik"
in Berichte/Analysen. Wien, Universal Edition [c1959], p. 50-58.
(Die Reihe: Information über serielle Musik, 5.)
        "Dieser Text diente als Vorlage zu einer Reihe von Vorlesungen
        an amerikanischen Universitäten im November 1958."
        A history of electronic music, general estimate of its possibili-
        ties, and description of its techniques.

270   Randolph, David. "A new music made with a machine," Horizon
      [New York] 1:50-55, 124-127 (Jan 1959). Illus., mus.
      A brief description of electronic music, musique concrète, and
      tape music; aesthetic considerations.

271   Winckel, Fritz. "Die Komposition mit elektroakustischen Mitteln,"
      NZfM 120:124-127 (Mar 1959). Illus.
      Brief description and history.

272   Walter, Arnold. "Music and electronics," Canadian music journal
      3:33-37 (Summer 1959).
      General description of the process of creating electronic music.
      Problem of totally predetermined music. The Cologne group.

COMPOSITIONAL TECHNIQUES

273   Meyer-Eppler, Werner. "Elektronische Kompositionstechnik," Melos
      20:5-9 (Jan 1953). Illus.
      Describes various electronic instruments and their use.

See no. 95 (Wörner, Karl H. "Neue Musik in der Entscheidung," 1954,
      p. 296-302).

274   Lindlar, Heinrich. "Elektronische Musik im Kölner Funkhaus,"
      Melos 21:326-327 (Nov 1954).
      A review of a concert of electronic music given in Cologne;
      includes a brief description of the technique used in composing
      electronic music.

275   Elektronische Musik. Wien, Universal Edition [c1955]. Hrsg. von
      Herbert Eimert unter Mitarbeit von Karlheinz Stockhausen. 63 p.
      Illus. (Die Reihe: Information über serielle Musik, 1.)

      Electronic music. Bryn Mawr, Pennsylvania, Theodore Presser
      [c1958]. vi + 62 p. Illus. (Die Reihe: a periodical devoted to devel-
      opments in contemporary music, ed. by Herbert Eimert and Karl-
      heinz Stockhausen, 1.)
          Contents of American edition: Translator's preface, vi; Eimert,
          Herbert, "What is electronic music?" p. 1-10; Stuckenschmidt,
          Hans Heinz, "The third stage: some observations on the aesthe-
          tics of electronic music," p. 11-13; Krenek, Ernst, "A glance
          over the shoulders of the young," p. 14-16 (see no. 50); Klebe,
          Giselher, "First practical work," p. 17-18; Boulez, Pierre, "'At
          the ends of the fruitful land . . .'" p. 19-29; Pousseur, Henri,
          "Formal elements in a new compositional material," p. 30-34;
          Goeyvaerts, Karol, "The sound material of electronic music,"
          p. 35-37; Gredinger, Paul, "Serial technique," p. 38-44; Stock-
          hausen, Karlheinz, "Actualia," p. 45-51; Koenig, Gottfried Michael,
          "Studio techniques," p. 52-54; Meyer-Eppler, Werner, "Statistic
          and psychologic problems of sound," p. 55-61 (includes a bibliog-
          raphy). (See no. 245.)

See no. 46 (Kelterborn, Rudolf. "Stilistisch gegensätzliche Entwicklungen auf der Basis der Zwölftontechnik," Apr 1956).

276   Le Caine, Hugh. "Electronic music," Proceedings of the Institute of Radio Engineers 44:457-478 (Apr 1956). Diagrs., illus.
   "New musical horizons through electronics," p. 475-478 (the musique concrète and Cologne groups). Technical and important article. Helpful bibliographical footnotes.

277   Enkel, Fritz. "Die Grundlagen der neuen Musik: das neue Klang-material (die Technik der elektronischen Klanggestaltung)," Grave-saner Blätter, Heft 6:20-27 (Dec 1956). Diagrs.
   Bibliography, p. 27; general article on the technique of electronic music.

278   Xénakis, Janis. "Wahrscheinlichkeitstheorie und Musik," Gravesaner Blätter, Heft 6:28-34 (Dec 1956). Diagrs.
   Highly technical article on the mathematical bases of electronic music.

279   Prieberg, Fred K. "Erste elektronische Partitur," NZfM 118:241 (Apr 1957).
   Stockhausen's Studie 2.

280   Van San, Hermann. "Einheitswissenschaft und Musik," Gravesaner Blätter, Heft 7/8:39-48 (Apr/May 1957). Diagrs.
   Highly technical article on "mathematical-electronic serial com-position"; includes a short bibliography.

See no. 261 (Becerra, Gustavo. "¿Que es la música electrónica?" Dec 1957).

281   Badings, Henk, and de Bruyn, J. W. "Electronic music," Philips technical review [English ed.] 19:191-201 (Dec 23, 1957). Diagrs., illus., mus.
   A 45 rpm phonorecord is included; it contains illustrations for the text and also an abridged version of Badings' ballet, Cain and Abel.
   Primarily an explanation of the method of procedure in compos-ing Bading's Cain and Abel ballet; various electronic techniques are described.

282   Wilkinson, Marc "Two months in the 'Studio di Fonologia,'" Score, no. 22:41-48 (Feb 1958).
   Brief, nontechnical account of techniques and equipment used in the Milan Studio. Definition of terms.

283   Koenig, Gottfried Michael. "Studium in Studio" in Berichte/Analysen. Wien, Universal Edition [c1959], p. 74-83. (Die Reihe: Information über serielle Musik, 5.)
   The teaching of electronic composition techniques.

See no. 272 (Walter, Arnold. "Music and electronics," Summer 1959).

*283a Prieberg, Fred K. Musica ex machina: über das Verhältnis von Musik und Technik. Berlin, Ullstein [1960]. 299 p.

III
THE VIENNESE SCHOOL

ARNOLD SCHOENBERG (1874-1951)

GENERAL
(Including Collections, Festschriften, etc.)

284   Arnold Schönberg. Mit Beiträgen von Alben Berg [et al.]. München, R. Piper, 1912. 90 p. Illus., mus.
> Partial contents: Webern, Anton, "Schönbergs Musik," p. 22-48 (brief discussion of early works with musical examples); also articles on Schoenberg as a painter and a teacher.

285   Rosenfeld, Paul. "Schoenberg" in his Musical portraits: interpretations of twenty modern composers. New York, Harcourt, Brace [c1920], p. 233-243.
> General; discusses works.

286   Wellesz, Egon. Arnold Schönberg. Leipzig, Tal & Co., 1921.

        ————. Arnold Schönberg. Tr. by W. H. Kerridge. London and New York, Dutton [1925]. vii + 159 p. Mus., port.
> Partial contents: "The new path," p. 10-39; "His teaching," p. 40-58; "His works," p. 59-154; "Chronological table," p. 155-156.
> Biography and discussion of his works, through the first twelve-tone works.

287   Gray, Cecil. "Arnold Schönberg, a critical study," M & L 3:73-89 (Jan 1922). Mus.
> Discussion of works (to 1921) and critical estimate.

288   Arnold Schönberg zum fünfzigsten Geburtstag, 13 September 1924. Wien [1924]. Mus., port. [Sonderheft der Musikblätter des Anbruch, Wien, 6:269-342 (Aug/Sept 1924).]
> Partial contents: Bekker, Paul, "Schönberg: 'Erwartung,'" p. 275-282; Stein, Erwin, "Neue Formenprinzipien," p. 286-303; Berg, Alban, "Warum ist Schönbergs Musik so schwer verständlich?" p. 329-341.
> Stein's article appears in English translation in his book, Orpheus in new guises (see no. 303); Berg's essay has been reprinted several times: in German (see no. 492); in English (see no. 470); in French (see no. 509).

289   *Stefan-Gruenfeldt, Paul. Arnold Schönberg, Wandlung-Legende-Erscheinung-Bedeutung. Wien, Zeitkunst Verlag [c1924]. 101 p.

"Arnold Schönbergs Werke," p. 102-103; "Literatur über Schönberg," p. 103.

290   Wellesz, Egon. "Arnold Schönberg: la voie nouvelle," Rev mus v. 7,
no. 6:12-25 (Apr 1926) and v. 7, no. 9:11-23 (Jul 1926). tr. by Stefan
Freund.

_____. "Arnold Schönberg: la doctrine," Rev mus v. 7, no. 10:126-
132 (Aug 1926) and v. 8, no. 1:38-46 (Jan 1927), tr. by Stefan Freund.
Schoenberg's life, works, and philosophy, to 1926.

291   Gray, Cecil. "Arnold Schönberg" in his A survey of contemporary
music. 2d ed. London, Oxford University Press, 1927, p. 162-183.
General discussion of works and style.

292   Mersmann, Hans. Die moderne Musik seit der Romantik. Wildpark-
Potsdam, Akademische Verlagsgesellschaft Athenaion [c1927]. Mus.,
illus.
Schoenberg, p. 132-143; Berg (especially Wozzeck), p. 144-147.
Brief analyses of works.

293   Arnold Schönberg zum 60. Geburtstag, 13 September 1934. [Wien,
Universal Edition, 1934?]. 75 p. Mus., port.
Partial contents: Webern, Anton, "Aus Schönbergs Schriften,"
p. 11-14; Hába, Alois, "Schönberg und die weiteren Möglichkeiten der Musikentwicklung," p. 15-17; Polnauer, Josef, "Schönbergs 'Verbundenheit,'" p. 44-49 (on the last of the six 'Stücken
für Männerchor,' op. 35); Broch, Hermann, "Irrationale Erkenntnis in der Musik," p. 49-60; Berg, Alban, "Glauben, Hoffnung un
Liebe," p. 61 (acrostic poem); "Verzeichnis der Werke von Arnold
Schönberg," p. 71-75.

294   *Sollertinskii, Ivan Ivanovich. Арнольд Шенберг. [Leningrad, Lenin-
gradskaiia Filarmonija, 1934]. 55 p.

See no. 78 (Wind, Hans E. Die Endkrise der bürgerlichen Musik und die
Rolle Arnold Schönberg, 1935).

295   Armitage, Merle, ed. Schoenberg. New York, G. Schirmer, 1937.
319 p. Illus.
Partial contents: Sessions, Roger, "Music in crisis," p. 9-39 (reprinted from Modern music; see no. 7); Weiss, Adolph, "The
twelve-tone series," p. 75-77 (written 1932); Krenek, Ernst,
"Arnold Schoenberg," p. 79-88; Saerchinger, César, "The truth
about Schoenberg," p. 89-107 (written 1930; discusses Schoenberg's works); Steuermann, Eduard, "The piano music of Schoenberg," p. 125-133; Viertel, Berthold, "Schoenberg's Jakobsleiter,"
p. 165-181; Pisk, Paul Amadeus, "Schoenberg's twelve-tone opera,"
p. 187-194 (reprinted from Modern music; see no. 488); Stefan,
Paul, "Schönberg's operas," p. 195-204 (reprinted from Modern
music; see no. 428); Slonimsky, Nicholas, "A Schoenberg chronol-
ogy [1874-1937]," p. 215-245; Schoenberg, Arnold, "Tonality and
form," p. 259-264 (reprinted from Pacific coast musician; see
no. 185); Schoenberg, Arnold, "Problems of harmony," p. 265-305
(reprinted from Modern music; see no. 184); list of works, p.
307-315.

See no. 81 (Hijman, Julius. Nieuwe oostenrijkse musiek, 1938).

296   Stefan, Paul. "Arnold Schoenberg" in Thompson, Oscar, ed. Great
      modern composers. New York, Dodd, Mead, 1941, p. 267-277.
      Biographical sketch and discussion of works; catalogue of Schoen-
      berg's works, p. 274-277.

297   Bauer, Marion. "Schoenberg and his innovation: atonality and twelve-
      tone technique" in her Twentieth century music. New ed. New York,
      Putnam [c1947], p. 207-230.
      Somewhat superficial but unbiased discussion of Schoenberg's
      life and works; also some mention of Berg, Webern, and Hauer.

298   Newlin, Dika. Bruckner, Mahler, Schoenberg. New York, King's
      Crown Press, 1947. 293 p. Mus.

      _____. Bruckner, Mahler, Schönberg. Übers. von C. Nameth und
      H. Zelzer. Wien, Bergland-Verlag, 1954. 303 p.
      A discussion of his life and works, to 1944.

See no. 84 (Leibowitz, René. "Arnold Schoenberg: the origin and founda-
      tions of contemporary music" in his Schoenberg and his school,
      1949, p. 43-134).

299   Wörner, Karl H. Musik der Gegenwart. Mainz, Schott [c1949].
      262 p. Illus., mus.
      Chapter 8: "Die jüngere Generations Gruppe des 'Tristan': Arnold
      Schönberg. Das Zwölftonmusik. Vom Wesen atonaler Musik," p.
      70-78; chapter 9: "Die Wiener atonale Schule: Alban Berg und
      Anton von Webern," p. 84-92.

300   The canon: Australian journal of music [Arnold Schoenberg jubilee
      issue]. v. 3, no. 2 (Sept 1949).
      Partial contents: Newlin, Dika, "Schoenberg's new 'Fantasy,'"
      p. 83-84; Leibowitz, René, "Arnold Schoenberg's recent tonal
      works and the synthesis of tonality," p. 86-90; Pisk, Paul, "Arnold
      Schoenberg—the influence of my musical youth," p. 94-96.

301   Stuckenschmidt, Hans Heinz. Arnold Schoenberg. Zürich, Atlantis
      [1951]. 126 p. Mus.

      _____. Arnold Schoenberg. Tr. de l'allemand par Alexandre von
      Spitzmüller et Claude Rostand. Monaco, Editions du Rocher [1956].
      182 p. Mus. (Domaine musical.)
      Contents of the French edition include: "Note sommaire sur le
      système dodécaphonique et la méthode sérielle, par Claude
      Rostand," p. 139-143; "Chronologie," p. 145-167; "Table des
      oeuvres d'Arnold Schönberg," p. 169-177; "Discographie," p. 179-
      182.

      _____. Arnold Schoenberg. Tr. by E. T. Roberts and Humphrey
      Searle. London, Calder [c1959]. 168 p. Illus, mus.
      Contents of the English edition include a letter to the author
      from Thomas Mann, and a list of Schoenberg's compositions
      (p. 161-163).

See no. 89 (Reich, Willi. "Versuch einer Geschichte der Zwölftonmusik"
      in Alte und neue Musik, 1952).

302 Searle, Humphrey. "Schoenberg and the future," Hinrichsen's musical yearbook 7:134-140 (1952). Mus., ports.
>   List of Schoenberg's works, p. 139-140. A brief summation of
>   Schoenberg's achievements and a discussion of some of his works.

303 Stein, Erwin. Orpheus in new guises. London, Rockliff [c1953].
vii + 167 p. Mus., ports.
>   Partial contents: "Mahler, Reger, Strauss and Schoenberg: some
>   observations on the technique of composition," p. 36-46 (reprinted
>   from the Jahrbuch 1926 der Universal Edition; see no. 381);
>   "Schoenberg," p. 47-54; "The Gurrelieder," p. 55-56 (from the
>   Christian Science Monitor, Oct 3, 1931); "New formal principles,"
>   p. 57-77 (reprinted from Arnold Schönberg zum fünfzigsten Geburts-
>   tag; see no. 288); "Some observations on Schoenberg's twelve-note
>   rows," p. 78-81 (reprinted from Anbruch; see no. 382); "Perform-
>   ing Schoenberg's music," p. 83-85 (first published as "Über der
>   Vortrag von Schönbergs Musik," Pult und Tagstock, Sept 1924);
>   "The treatment of the speaking voice in 'Pierrot Lunaire,'" p. 86-
>   80 (published as "Die Behandlung der Sprechstimme in 'Pierrot
>   Lunaire,'" in Pult und Tagstock, Mar/Apr 1927); "Musical thought:
>   Beethoven and Schoenberg," p. 90-95 (reprinted from Anbruch;
>   see no. 383); "Anton Webern—Obituary," p. 99-102 (from MT; see
>   no. 565); "Wozzeck," p. 103-107 (reprinted from Opera; see no.
>   553); "Berg's opera Lulu in Zürich," p. 108-109 (from the Chris-
>   tian Science Monthly, July 13, 1937).
>   A useful collection of many of his articles which have appeared
>   in various publications; several of these writings are here trans-
>   lated into English for the first time.

See no. 94 (Rognoni, Luigi. Espressionismo e dodecafonia, 1954).

304 Searle, Humphrey. "Schoenberg, Arnold" in Grove's Dictionary of
music and musicians. 5th ed. London, Macmillan, 1954, v. 7:513-523.
>   Extensive bibliography. Includes a list of his works. Article is
>   arranged into three parts: life, compositions, summary.

See no. 100 (Collaer, Paul. La musique moderne, 1905-1955. 1955, p. 35-
77).

See no. 569 (Metzger, Heinz Klaus. "Webern and Schönberg" in Anton
Webern, 1955, p. 42-45 [Die Reihe, 2]).

See no. 105 (Goehr, Walter. "Arnold Schönberg's development towards
the twelve-note system" in Hartog, Howard, ed. European music,
1957).

305 Magnani, Luigi. Le frontiere della musica, da Monteverdi a Schoenberg. Milano, Ricciardi, 1957, 328 p. Mus.
>   Partial contents: "Insegnamento di Schoenberg," p. 191-217 (written
>   in 1947; discusses early influences on Schoenberg and expression-
>   ism); "Schoenberg e la sua scuola," p. 218-226 (written in 1947;
>   discusses Leibowitz's book of that name; see no. 84).

See no. 112 (Prieberg, Fred K. "Arnold Schoenberg" in his Lexikon der
neuen Musik, 1958, p. 381-392).

See no. 116 (Vlad, Roman. Storia della dodecafonia, 1958).

306   Stuckenschmidt, Hans Heinz. "Stil und Ästhetik Schönbergs," Schw
       MZ 98:97-104 (Mar 1958).
            Lecture, given in Basel on Dec 14, 1957; reprinted in his Schöp-
            fer der neuen Musik (see no. 115).
            Schoenberg's musical philosophy; his harmonic language; bio-
            graphical-aesthetic sketch and discussion of works. An important
            article.

306a   Adorno, Theodor Wiesengrund. "Zur Vorgeschichte der Reihenkom-
       position" in his Klangfiguren. Berlin, Suhrkamp Verlag, c1959, p.
       95-120. (His Musikalische Schriften, I.)
            "Vortrag für den Nordeutschen Rundfunk 1958, unter Benutzung
            eines Aufsatzes über die Orchesterstücke op. 16 aus dem Schön-
            bergheft von 'Pult und Taktstock," März/April 1927. Ungedruckt."

See no. 118a (Zillig, Winfried. "Schönberg und sein Weg von der Tonalität
       zum Zwölftonsystem" in his Variationen über neue Musik, 1959).
            Contents: "Letzte Steigerung der Romantik und erste Anzeichen
            der Zeitenwende," p. 61-69; "An die Grenzen der Tonalität," p. 69-
            75; "Der absolute Umsturz," p. 75-83; "Die neue Gesetzmässigkeit
            des Zwölftonsystems," p. 83-94; "Rückkehr zur Tonalität?" p. 94-
            100; "Schönberg als politischer und religiöser Komponist," p. 100-
            107.

PHILOSOPHY AND CRITICISM

307   Newman, Ernest. "A propos of Schönberg's Five orchestral pieces,"
       MT 55:87-89 (Feb 1, 1914).
            A critical estimate of Schoenberg as a composer. Appended are
            excerpts from program notes on the Orchestral pieces, written
            by a Mrs. Newmarch.

308   Calvocoressi, M. D. "The classicism of Arnold Schönberg," MT
       55:234-236 (Apr 1, 1914). Mus.
            Schoenberg's musical philosophy and classical background.

309   Bekker, Paul. Kritische Zeitbilder. Berlin, Schuster & Loeffler,
       1921. 336 p.
            Essays on composers and aspects of music. "Schönberg," p. 161-
            173, is a general discussion of Schoenberg's style.

310   Bücken, Ernst. Führer und Probleme der neuen Musik. Köln,
       Tonger, 1924. 172 p. Mus.
            "Impressionismus und Expressionismus," p. 126-163. (Schoen-
            berg, p. 149-163.) Examples from his op. 11 and 15, and Pierrot.

311   Stein, Erwin. "Schoenberg and the German line," Modern music
       3:22-27 (May 1926).
            Schoenberg seen as a continuation of the tradition of German
            music.

312   Cort Van den Linden, R. "Arnold Schoenberg," M & L 7:322-331
       (Oct 1926) and 8:38-45 (Jan 1927), tr. by Scott Goddard. Mus.
            A discussion of Schoenberg's personality and early works.

313   Stein, Erwin. "Idées d'Arnold Schönberg sur la musique," Rev mus
      10:1-6 (Nov 1928), tr. by J. Peyraube.
         In the form of a dialogue between Schoenberg and Stein.

See no. 3 (Adorno, Theodor Wiesengrund. "Zur Zwölftontechnik," Sept/Oct
1929).

314   Collaer, Paul. "Le cas Schoenberg," Revue international de la
      musique [Brussels] 1:432-440 (July/Sept 1938).
         An attack on Schoenberg as a "cerebral" composer.

315   Feldman, Harry Allen. "Futurism—Arnold Schoenberg" in his Music
      and the listener. New York, Dutton, 1939, p. 169-182.
         A rather general, anti-Schoenberg article.

316   Stein, Erwin. "Schoenberg's position today," Christian Science Moni-
      tor, v. 32, no. 1:9 (Nov 25, 1939).
         An evaluation of Schoenberg's music and of the twelve-tone tech-
      nique.

317   Taylor, Noel Heath. "Arnold Schoenberg: music in motion," Etc.:
      a review of general semantics 2:1-9 (Autumn 1944).
         A general semanticist's view of criticisms of Schoenberg's music
      and of atonality in general.

318   Graf, Max. "Modern music in Vienna: Richard Strauss, Gustav Mah-
      ler, Arnold Schönberg" in his Legend of a musical city. New York,
      Philosophical library, 1945, p. 193-220.
         General Zeitgeist.

319   Graf, Max. "The path of Arnold Schoenberg" in his Modern music:
      music and composers of our time. Tr. by Beatrice R. Maier. New
      York, Philosophical Library [c1946], p. 168-196.
         Contains a great many sweeping generalities.

320   Leibowitz, René. "Innovation and tradition in contemporary music:
      I: The traditional significance of the music of Arnold Schoenberg,"
      Horizon [London] 15:55-63 (Jan 1947).
         Schoenberg seen as a traditional composer. This article, written
      from an historical viewpoint, attempts to summarize the "princi-
      ples which determine the character and evolution of Schoenberg's
      music."

See no. 13 (Adorno, Theodor Wiesengrund. "Schönberg und der Fortschnitt"
in his Philosophie der neuen Musik, 1949, p. 19-88).

321   Mitchell, Donald. "Schoenberg the traditionalist," Chesterian 24:1-6
      (Jul 1949).
         Schoenberg as a romanticist; discussion of his works.

322   Eimert, Herbert. "Arnold Schönberg, der Fünfundsiebzig-Jährige,"
      Melos 16:226-230 (Sept 1949). Port.
         Essay in honor of Schoenberg's 75th birthday; general evaluation
      of his works and importance.

323   Wörner, Karl H. "Arnold Schönberg: zu seinem 75. Geburtstag am
      13. September," Musica 3:310-312 (Sept 1949).
         Schoenberg's work, accomplishments, and influence.

324   Marcel, Luc-André. "Arnold Schoenberg," Cahiers du Sud [Paris],
      v. 34, no. 308:130-136 (1951).
      Obituary; estimation of his achievements.

325   Salazar, Adolfo. "Arnold Schoenberg post-mortem: ad usum Del-
      phini," Nuestra musica, v. 6, no. 2:202-221 (1951).
      Topics discussed: "Schoenberg y el atonalismo"; "Naturaleza y
      convencion en la tonalidad"; "Los principios milenarios de la
      tonalidad"; "Los griegos"; "El superrealismo, las concordancias
      vizcaínas y otros 'scherzi'"; "Los expresionistas"; "La escuela
      de las dos sonidos."
      A general and nontechnical article.

326   "Notes of the day," Mo mus rec 81:169-170 (Sept 1951) and 81:198-
      199 (Oct 1951).
      Obituary and quite biased attack on Schoenberg as a composer
      "more intellectual than musical." A reply to this by Humphrey
      Searle is included in:

      _____. Mo mus rec 82:3 (Jan 1952).

327   Reich, Willi. "Arnold Schönberg (1874-1951)," Schw MZ 91:354-355
      (Sept 1951).
      Obituary; summary of his life, works, and philosophy.

328   Reich, Willi. "Freiwillige für Schoenberg," Melos 18:246-248 (Sept
      1951).
      Obituary; Schoenberg's influence on the musical world; the im-
      portance of the twelve-tone technique.

329   "Arnold Schoenberg, 1874-1951," M & L 32:305-323 (Oct 1951).
      A collection of brief and largely unfavorable statements about
      Schoenberg's music, by various people. (See no. 330.)

330   Neighbour, Oliver W. "In defense of Schönberg," M & L 33:10-27
      (Jan 1952). Mus.
      A reply to the Schoenberg symposium in M & L (see no. 320).
      Schoenberg's relation to musical tradition; tonality in his music;
      his harmonic vocabulary; a discussion of his works.

331   Duhamel, Antoine. "Arnold Schoenberg, la critique, et le monde
      musical contemporain" in L'oeuvre du XXe siècle. Paris, Richard-
      Masse, April 1952, p. 77-85. (La revue musicale, no. 212.)
      Schoenberg and musical criticism.

332   Boulez, Pierre. "Schoenberg is dead," Score, no. 6:18-22 (May 1952).
      Weaknesses in Schoenberg's development of the twelve-tone tech-
      nique, as seen from the "post-Webern" point of view. Has been
      an influential article.

333   Glock, William. "Comment," Score, no. 6:3-6 (May 1952).
      An appraisal of Schoenberg and the twelve-note technique.

334   Goldbeck, Fred. "The strange case of Schönberg, revolutionary
      composer and tradition-abiding musician," Score, no. 6:36-39 (May
      1952).
      Schoenberg and the romantic tradition.

335   Keller, Hans. "The B.B.C.'s victory over Schoenberg," Mus rev
       13:130-132 (May 1952).
           Comment on the M & L symposium (see no. 329) and on the
           B.B.C.'s Third Programme series on Schoenberg.

336   Martin, Frank. "Schoenberg and ourselves," Score, no. 6:15-17
       (May 1952). Ports.
           French translation in Le systeme dodécaphonique (see no. 141).
           Twelve-tone technique seen as an enrichment of composers'
           musical means.

337   Sessions, Roger. "Some notes on Schönberg and the 'method of
       composing with twelve tones,'" Score, no. 6:7-10 (May 1952).
           Significance of the twelve-tone technique.

338   Wörner, Karl H. "Der unbekannte Schönberg," Melos 19:342-344
       (Dec 1952).
           Schoenberg a relatively unknown composer in Europe at the
           time of his death, because of few performances.

See no. 27 (Pfrogner, Hermann. Die Zwölfordnung der Töne, 1953).

339   Adorno, Theodor Wiesengrund. "Arnold Schönberg, 1874-1951," Die
       neue Rundschau 64:80-104 (1953).
           Characteristics of his music and aesthetics; some problems
           inherent in the twelve-tone technique.

340   Pincherle, Marc. "Aspects de Schoenberg," Schw MZ 93:158-160
       (Apr 1953).
           Some aspects of Schoenberg's character.

341   Mitchell, Donald. "Bartók, Stravinsky, and Schoenberg: periods
       early, middle and late," Chesterian 28:9-16 (Jul 1953).
           Schoenberg, p. 14 10; concerns the implications of Schoenberg's
           "reversion" to tonality in some of his later works.

342   Pannain, Guido. "Schönberg e la 'Filosofia della musica nuova,'"
       Rass mus 23:193-209 (Jul 1953).
           Refers to Adorno's book (see no. 13).

See no. 29 (Goléa, Antoine. Esthétique de la musique contemporaine,
       1954, p. 48-52, 56-63).

343   Citkowitz, Israel. "Stravinsky and Schoenberg: a note on syntax
       and sensibility," Juilliard review 1:17-20 (Fall 1954).
           A comparison of the philosophies of Schoenberg and Stravinsky;
           their reasons for using serial techniques.

See no. 35 (Vlad, Roman. "Elementi metafisici nella poetica schönberghi-
       ana" in his Modernità e tradizione nella musica contemporanea,
       1955, p. 185-196).

344   Eisler, Hanns. "Arnold Schönberg," Sinn und Form [Berlin] 7:5-15
       (1955).
           General essay; discussion of stylistic elements of Schoenberg's
           "Three periods"; problems of the twelve-tone technique (see
           nos. 345 and 346).

See no. 37 (Adorno, Theodor Wiesengrund. "Zum Verständnis Schönbergs," Jun 1955).

345   Laux, Karl. "'Die moderne Musik ist tot'—in Amerika und anderswo —in der D. D. R. feiert sie frölich Urständ," Musik und Gesellschaft [E. Berlin] 5:212-217 (Jul 1955).
      Claims "decadent bourgeois contemporary music" is dead; attacks Eisler's pro-Schoenberg article (no. 344) on Marxist grounds.

346   Rubin, Marcel. "Was bedeutet uns Schönberg? Eine Antwort an Hanns Eisler," Musik und Gesellschaft [E. Berlin] 5:274-275 (Sept 1955).
      Another attack on Eisler's article (see nos. 344 and 345).
      Compares Schoenberg (unfavorably) with Beethoven, Schubert, Mahler, and Janáček. Finds Schoenberg's music meaningless.

347   Bentzon, Niels Viggo. "Omkring Arnold Schønberg," Dansk Musiktidsskrift 31:9-13 (Feb 1956). Port.
      Serial technique; Schoenberg's works and philosophy.

348   Burt, Francis. "An antithesis: the technical aspect," Score, no. 18:7-17 (Dec 1956).

      _____. "An antithesis; the aesthetic aspect," Score, no. 19:60-74 (Mar 1957).
      Reconciliation of the Stravinsky-Schoenberg antithesis.

349   Mellers, Wilfred Howard. "Schoenberg and Hindemith" in his Romanticism and the twentieth century. Fair Lawn, N. J., Essential books, 1957, p. 182-193. Mus.
      A general essay on Schoenberg's and Berg's "style" and the twelve-tone technique.

350   Keller, Hans. "The new in review: Schönberg—I: the problem of performance," Mus rev 18:150-153 (May 1957).
      Critical comments, especially about critics.

351   Skrebkow, S. "Gegen die Atonalität Schönbergs, für Prokofjew. Einige Forderungen an die Musikästhetik," Sowjetwissenschaft; Kunst und Literatur [E. Berlin] 5:486-495 (May 1957). Mus.
      A "socialist realist" interpretation of melody in Prokofief, Schoenberg, and other composers. (None of the musical examples is from Schoenberg.)

See no. 56 (Melichar, Alois. Musik in der Zwangsjacke, 1958).

352   Wolff, Helmut Christian. "Palestrina und Schönberg—zwei Extreme der europäischen Musik" in Bericht über den Internationalen Musikwissenschaftlichen Kongress, Wien; Mozartjahr 1956; hrsg. von Erich Schenk. Graz, Hermann Böhlaus, 1958, p. 749-753.
      An aesthetically oriented comparison of Palestrina and Schoenberg.

353   Keller, Hans. "Moses, Freud, and Schönberg," Mo mus rec 88:12-16 (Jan/Feb 1958) and 88:63-67 (Mar/Apr 1958).
      The relationship (or lack of relationship) between Freud and Schoenberg; their attitudes toward religion; their interpretation of Moses.

See no. 306 (Stuckenschmidt, Hans Heinz. "Stil und Asthetik Schönbergs," Mar 1958).

354   Blanks, Fred. "Arnold Schoenberg," Canon 11:273-276 (Mar/Apr 1958). Port.
       Brief biographical sketch. Discusses the Jewish element in Schoenberg's musik.

See no. 378 (Schoenberg, Arnold, "Aus Briefen Arnold Schönbergs," Dec 1958).

BIOGRAPHY

See no. 284 (Arnold Schönberg. Mit Beiträgen von Alban Berg [et al.], 1912).

355   Maclean, Charles. "London notes," Zeitschrift der Internationalen Musikgesellschaft 15:129-132 (Feb 1914).
       An interesting contemporary account of Schoenberg's difficulties in getting performances, and some (biased) comments on Schoenberg's music.

356   Maclean, Charles. "Schönberg: a short sketch of his life," MT 55:302-304 (May 1, 1914).
       An account of the dates of Schoenberg's compositions and their performances; some bibliographical data (on reviews) included. "From the Journal of the International Music Society, with additions." (See no. 355.)

357   Schoenberg, Arnold. "Mein Publikum," Der Querschnitt 10:222-224 (Apr 1930).
       Reaction of the public to Schoenberg's works.

358   Bach, David Joseph. "A note on Arnold Schoenberg," MQ 22:8-13 (Jan 1936).
       Biographical sketch: influences on Schoenberg.

359   Milhaud, Darius. "To Arnold Schoenberg on his 70th birthday: personal reflections," MQ 30:379-385 (Oct 1944). Port.
       Reminiscences by Milhaud relating to Schoenberg's music.

360   Leibowitz, René. "Music chronicle; two composers: a letter from Hollywood," Partisan review 15:361-365 (Mar 1948).
       On Schoenberg and Stravinsky; Schoenberg's life in California, to 1947.

361   Newlin, Dika. "Schönberg in America, 1933-1948; retrospect and prospect," Mus sur, v. 1, no. 5:128-131 (1949) and v. 1, no. 6:185-189 (1949). Mus.
       Biographical; description of his "American" works; discussion of his ideas.

362   Schoenberg, Arnold. "Further to the Schoenberg-Mann controversy," Mus sur 2:77-80 (Autumn, 1949), tr. by Hans Keller.
       One of several articles dealing with the controversy between Schoenberg and Thomas Mann over Mann's book Doktor Faustus.

363   Leibowitz, René. "Besuch bei Arnold Schönberg," Schw MZ 89:324-
328 (Sept 1949).
"Zum 75. Geburtstag des Komponisten."
Various remarks on the author's experiences with Schoenberg.

364   Schoenberg, Arnold. "Mia evolución," Nuestra musica 4:239-249
(Oct 1949).

_____. "My evolution," MQ 38:517-527 (Oct 1952).
Autobiographical essay; his discovery of the "method of composing with twelve tones."

365   Foss, Hubert. "Schoenberg, 1874-1951," MT 92:401-403 (Sept 1951).
Obituary. Contains useful biographical data, including dates of
some performances. Some of the information is inaccurate,
however, and should be used with caution.

366   Rubsamen, Walter H. "Schoenberg in America," MQ 37:469-489
(Oct 1951). Illus.

_____. "Schoenberg in Amerika," Melos 20:132-137 (May 1953)
and 20:168-173 (Jun 1953).
Biographical and anecdotal account of Schoenberg's years in
America, 1933-1951.

367   Robbins, Michela. "A Schoenberg seminar," Counterpoint 17:9-12
(Feb 1952). Port.
An informal discussion, by some of his pupils, of Schoenberg
as composer and teacher.

368   Newlin, Dika. "Arnold Schönberg in Amerika," ÖMZ 7:160-163
(May/Jun 1952).
Biographical sketch and list of works, 1935-1951; brief discussion of the row technique of his Piano concerto. (Not the same
article as her "Schönberg in America, 1933-1948"; see no. 361.)

369   Schoenberg, Arnold. "A self-analysis," Musical America 73:14, 172
(Feb 1953). Port.
A brief self-justification. Posthumous MS.

370   Milhaud, Darius. "Begegnungen mit Schönberg," Melos 22:100-103
(Apr 1955).
Dialogue between Claude Rostand and Darius Milhaud, on Schoen-
berg and the twelve-tone technique.

371   Milhaud, Darius. "Erinnerungen am Arnold Schönberg," ÖMZ 10:406-
410 (Dec 1955).
Further reminiscences. (See also no. 359.)

See no. 508 (Reich, Willi. "Alban Berg als Apologet Arnold Schönbergs,"
Dec 1955).

See no. 376 (Schoenberg, Arnold. Briefe, 1958, p. 13-14, 59-60, 121-122,
193-194, 241-242).

372   Ketting, Otto. "Arnold Schönberg in Amerika," Mens en melodie
13:79-81 (Mar 1958). Port.
Very brief; discusses works written during Schoenberg's American
period.

CORRESPONDENCE

See no. 390 (Schoenberg, Arnold [Letter to Nicolas Slonimsky], in Norman, Gertrude, ed., Letters of composers, 1946).

373   Keller, Hans, ed. and tr., "Unpublished Schoenberg letters, early, middle and late," Mus sur 4:449-471 (Jun 1952).
Letters to Marietta Werndorff, Erwin Stein, Oscar Adler, and Humphrey Searle.

374   Hill, Richard S. "Annual reports on acquisitions: music," Library of Congress quarterly journal of current acquisitions 10:43-44 (Nov 1952).
A report of the acquisition of the correspondence of Berg, Schoenberg, and Webern.

See no. 192 (Yasser, Joseph, "A letter from Arnold Schoenberg," Spring 1953).

See no. 514 (Rufer, Josef, "Dokumente einer Freundschaft," Feb 1955).

See no. 444 (Reich, Willi, "Ein Briefwechsel über 'Moses und Aron,'" Jun 1957).

375   Birke, Joachim. "Richard Dehmel und Arnold Schönberg; ein Briefwechsel," Die Musikforschung 11:279-285 (1958).

376   Schoenberg, Arnold. Briefe. Ausgewählt und hrsg. von Erwin Stein. Mainz, Schott, 1958.   309 p.
Letters written from 1910-1951.
Biographical data, p. 13-14, 59-60, 121-122, 193-194, 241-242.
Index of works, p. 15, 60, 122, 195, 242. Has a name and subject index.

See no. 581 (Gerhard, Roberto, ed. "Letters of Webern and Schoenberg," Nov 1958).

377   Schoenberg, Arnold. "Briefe aus vier Jahrzehnten," Melos 25:352-356 (Nov 1958).
These letters also appear in no. 376.

378   [Schoenberg, Arnold]. "Aus Briefen Arnold Schönbergs," NZfM 119:700-705 (Dec 1958).   Illus.
"Die nachfolgen Auszüge beschränken sich auf Grundsätzliches über ästhetische Fragen, Werke, und Aufführungen."
These letters also appear in no. 376.

379   [Schoenberg, Arnold]. "Ein unbekannter Brief von Arnold Schönberg an Alban Berg," ÖMZ 14:10 (Jan 1959).

COMPOSITIONAL TECHNIQUES

380   Somigli, Carlo. "Il modus operandi di Arnold Schoenberg," Riv mus
      ital 20:583-606 ([Jul/Sept] 1913). Mus.
      Discussion of Alaleona's theories of atonality (see nos. 176-177);
      discussion of Schoenberg's techniques in op. 6, 10, 11, and other
      works.

381   Stein, Erwin. "Mahler, Reger, Strauss und Schönberg; Kompositions-
      technische Betrachtungen" in 25. Jahre neue Musik: Jahrbuch 1926
      der Universal Edition. Wien, Universal Edition, 1926, p. 63-78.
      English translation in his Orpheus in new guises (see no. 303).
      Schoenberg, p. 74-78; résumé of his composition technique.

382   Stein, Erwin. "Einige Bemerkungen zu Schönbergs Zwölftonreihen,"
      Anbruch 8:251-253 (Jun/Jul 1926).
      On the development of the twelve-tone technique by Schoenberg.
      English translation in his Orpheus in new guises (see no. 303).

383   Stein, Erwin. "Das gedankliche Prinzip in Beethovens Musik und
      seine Auswirkung bei Schönberg," Anbruch 9:117-121 (Mar 1927).
      Mus.
      The influence of Beethoven's style on Schoenberg. English trans-
      lation in his Orpheus in new guises (see no. 303).

384   Westphal, Kurt. "Arnold Schönbergs Weg zur Zwölftonmusik: zu-
      gleich ein Beitrag zur Entwicklungsgeschichte der modernen Musik,"
      Die Musik 21:491-499 (Apr 1929). Mus.
      The development of Schoenberg's serial technique; some analyti-
      cal examples from his op. 25 and 26.

385   Weiss, Adolf. "The lyceum of Schönberg," Modern music 9:99-107
      (Mar/Apr 1932).
      A codification of the compositional practices of Schoenberg, in
      general terms.

386   Hill, Richard S. "Schoenberg's tone-rows and the tonal system of
      the future," MQ 22:14-37 (Jan 1936). Mus., port.
      An important article. Traces the development of the twelve-tone
      technique; illustrates types of row structure used in various
      works of Schoenberg. Includes some bibliographical citations.

See no. 186 (Taylor, Noel Heath. "The Schoenberg concept," Apr 1939).

387   Krenek, Ernst. "Homage to Schönberg: the idiom and the technique,"
      Modern music 21:131-134 (Mar/Apr 1944). Port.
      Dodecaphony compared with "atonality"; implications of the
      twelve-tone technique.

388   Jalowetz, Heinrich. "On the spontaneity of Schoenberg's music,"
      MQ 30:385-408 (Oct 1944). Mus.
      The importance of melodic invention in Schoenberg's music;
      his Piano concerto is discussed in particular.

See no. 137 (Eschman, Karl. Changing forms in modern music, 1945,
      p. 104-110).

389   Katz, Adele T. Challenge to musical tradition: a new concept of
      tonality. New York, Knopf, 1945. Mus.
          "Schoenberg," p. 350-397.
          An attempt to extend Heinrich Schenker's system of analysis to
          non-tonal music. Discusses Schoenberg's Verklärte Nacht, D
          minor quartet, Kammersymphonie op. 9, F minor quartet, Three
          piano pieces, op. 11, and Suite for piano, op. 25. Also takes up
          problems of "tonality vs. atonality" and "dissonance."

390   Schoenberg, Arnold. [Letter to Nicolas Slonimsky] in Norman,
      Gertrude, ed. Letters of composers. New York, Knopf, 1946,
      p. 341-342.
          Describes briefly Schoenberg's development of the twelve-note
          technique.

391   Wood, Ralph W. "Concerning 'Sprechgesang,'" Tempo, no. 17 [no. 2
      of new series]:3-6 (Dec 1946). Mus.
          Sprechstimme in Schoenberg's and Berg's vocal works.

See no. 143 (Schoenberg, Arnold. "Composition with twelve tones" in his
      Style and idea, 1950).

392   Perle, George. "Schönberg's late style," Mus rev 13:274-282 (Nov
      1952).
          Row structure in Schoenberg's last works; an important article.
          A reply to this by Hans Keller is included in no. 28.

See no. 154 (Erickson, Robert. The structure of music, 1955).

See no. 43 (Rochberg, George. "Tradition and twelve-tone music," Dec
      1955 ?).

See no. 103 (Gottschalk, Nathan. Twelve-note music as developed by
      Arnold Schoenberg, 1956).

See no. 160 (Perle, George. Serial composition and atonality, 1956).

See no. 348 (Burt, Francis. "An antithesis: the technical aspect," Dec
      1956).

See no. 586 (Pousseur, Henri. "Da Schoenberg a Webern," Dec 1956).

393   Wellesz, Egon. The origins of Schönberg's twelve-tone system.
      Washington, D.C., 1958. 14 p. Mus.
          "A lecture delivered in the Whittall Pavilion of the Library of
          Congress, January 10, 1957."
          The musical influences upon Schoenberg; his development of the
          twelve-tone technique.

394   Walker, Alan. "Schönberg's classical background," Mus rev 19:283-
      289 (Nov 1958). Mus.
          Schoenbergian techniques derived from Mozart and Beethoven.

GENERAL DESCRIPTIONS OF WORKS

See no. 467 (Wellesz, Egon. "Arnold Schönberg," Sept 1911).

See no. 380 (Somigli, Carlo. "Il modus operandi di Arnold Schoenberg," [Jul-Sept] 1913).

395   Wellesz, Egon. "Schönberg and beyond," MQ 2:76-95 (Jan 1916), tr. by Otto Kinkeldey. Mus.
        Brief biographical sketch. Primarily a discussion of his works, especially the Songs, op. 1-3, Gurrelieder, second String quartet, and George songs.

396   Wellesz, Egon. "Arnold Schönberg et son oeuvre," Rev mus 4:1-18 (May 1923). Mus.
        Early works, through op. 22.

See no. 312 (Cort Van den Linden, R. "Arnold Schoenberg," Oct 1926).

See no. 181 (Erpf, Hermann Robert. Studien zur Harmonie- und Klang-technik, 1927).

397   Wellesz, Egon. "Schoenberg, Arnold" in Cobbett, Walter W. Cobbett's cyclopedic survey of chamber music. London, Oxford University Press, 1929-30, v. 2:343-352. Mus.
        Brief discussion of the sextet Verklärte Nacht; the first, second, and third String quartets; the first Chamber symphony; Pierrot Lunaire; the Serenade, op. 24; the Wind quintet; and the Suite, op. 29.

398   Harrison, Lou. "Homage to Schonberg: the late works," Modern music 21:135-138 (Mar/Apr 1944).
        The Piano concerto, the Violin concerto, and the fourth String quartet; row structures of the middle and late periods compared.

See no. 141 (Leibowitz, René. "Aspects récents de la technique de douze sons" in Le système dodécaphonique, 1949, p. 32-53).
        On three works of Schoenberg: the Prélude, op. 44; the String trio, op. 45; the Survivor from Warsaw, op. 46.

See no. 361 (Newlin, Dika. "Schönberg in America," 1949).

See no. 300 (Leibowitz, René. "Arnold Schoenberg's recent tonal works" in The canon: Arnold Schoenberg jubilee issue, Sept 1949).

399   Vlad, Roman. "L'ultimo Schönberg," Rass mus 21:106-116 (Apr 1951). Mus.
        A discussion of the works through the String trio, op. 45, and the Survivor from Warsaw. Reprinted in Vlad's Modernità e tradizione nella musica contemporanea, p. 158-173 (see no. 35).

400   Keller, Hans. "Schoenberg," Mus sur 3:277-285 (June 1951).
        Discusses the Survivor from Warsaw, the Fantasy for violin, and Schoenberg's book, Style and idea (see no. 143).

401   Stephan, Rudolph. "Unorthodoxe Musik: dem Künstler und Menschen Arnold Schönberg zum Gedachtnis," Dt Univ Zt 6, no. 15/16:16-18 (July 1951). Mus.
       Obituary and discussion of his last works.

402   Redlich, Hans F. "Arnold Schönberg," Mus rev 12:304-306 (Nov 1951). Mus.
       Obituary and discussion of works.

403   Demuth, Norman. Musical trends in the twentieth century. London, Rockliff [c1952]. Illus., mus.
       Biographical sketches and discussion of works. Some row analysis.
       Partial contents: "Arnold Schoenberg," p. 209-232; "Anton von Webern," p. 233-238; "Alban Berg," p. 239-245.

404   Rankle, Karl. "Arnold Schönberg," Score, no. 6:40-43 (May 1952). Mus.
       A very brief discussion of Schoenberg's works, especially the Jakobsleiter, by a former Schoenberg pupil.

405   Keller, Hans. "Concerts and opera: Schoenberg memorial concert," Mus rev 13:216-218 (Aug 1952). Mus.
       A lively review of Schoenberg's three Songs, op. 48, the Suite, and the fourth Quartet.

406   "Catalogue des oeuvres d'Arnold Schoenberg (1874-1951)," Music information record, no. 11:12-15 (winter 1953/54).
       Includes his transcriptions and theoretical writings.

See no. 95 (Wörner, Karl H. Neue Musik in der Entscheidung, 1954, p. 56-67).
       Musical examples from Schoenberg's Survivor from Warsaw, String trio, and Erwartung. Description of works and style.

See no. 155 (Ogden, Wilbur Lee. Series and structure, 1955).

407   Stuckenschmidt, Hans Heinz. "Schönbergs religiöse Werke," Schw MZ 97:256-258 (June 1957).
       Survey of Gurrelieder, Jakobsleiter, Moses und Aron, Moderne Psalmen, Kol Nidre, Survivor from Warsaw, and other religious works by Schoenberg.

408   "Notas del extranjero; Alemania: el legado de Schoenberg," Revista musicale chilena 12:80-81 (Jan/Feb 1958).
       A brief description of a concert which presented several unpublished and previously unperformed works of Schoenberg.

409   Koegler, Horst. "The international scene: Germany," Musical courier 157:29 (Feb 1958).
       Another brief account of the performance of Schoenberg's unpublished works.

410   Rufer, Josef. "A talk on Arnold Schoenberg," Score, no. 22:7-11 (Feb 1958), tr. by Paul Hamburger.
       A discussion of Schoenberg's unpublished works. Originally presented as a talk at the Berlin Akademie der Künste.

411 Rufer, Josef. "Arnold Schönbergs Nachlass," ÖMZ 13:96-106 (Mar 1958). Illus., port.
A description of Schoenberg's unpublished works: documents, notebooks, compositions.

412 Rufer, Josef. Das Werk Arnold Schönbergs. Kassel, Bärenreiter, 1959. xii + 207 p. Illus., facsim.
A complete and handsomely printed catalogue of Schoenberg's works. Contents: 1. Music (published and unpublished, including sketchbooks); 2. Writings (theoretical, poetical, articles, etc.); 3. Paintings (includes 10 plates); 4. Chronological list of works and first performances.

413 Gradenwitz, Peter. "Schönbergs religiöse Werke," Melos 11:330-333 (Nov 1959).
English translation: "The religious works of Arnold Schönberg," Mus rev 21:19-29 (Feb 1960). Mus.
A brief discussion of Schoenberg's religious philosophy as expressed in Moses und Aron, Jakobsleiter, Moderne Psalmen, Kol Nidre, and other works.

INDIVIDUAL WORKS

Das Buch der hängenden Gärten, op. 15
See his Songs—op. 15

Chamber symphony, op. 9
See his Kammersymphonie, op. 9

Choral works
—op. 13 (Friede auf Erden)

414 Guenther, Siegfried. "Das trochäische Prinzip in Arnold Schoenbergs op. 13: Versuch einer Grundlage zur stilkritischen Erfassung seines gesamten Schaffens," Zeitschrift für Musikwissenschaft 6:158-176 (Dec 1923). Mus.
A somewhat statistical analysis.

—op. 27 (Four pieces for mixed chorus)

415 Stein, Erwin. "Neue Chöre von Schönberg," Anbruch 8:421-423 (Dec 1926).
Review (not an analysis) of op. 27 and 28.

416 Adorno, Theodor Wiesengrund. "Arnold Schönberg: Chöre op. 27 und op. 28," Anbruch 10:411-412 (Nov/Dec 1928).
Brief descriptive review.

—op. 28 (Three satires for mixed chorus)

See no. 415 (Stein, Erwin, "Neue Chöre von Schönberg," Dec 1926).

See no. 416 (Adorno, Theodor Wiesengrund. "Arnold Schönberg: Chöre," Nov/Dec 1928).

—op. 35 (Six pieces for male chorus)

417   Reich, Willi. "Schönberg's new Männerchor," Modern music 9:62-66 (Jan/Feb 1932). Mus.
A discussion of the structure of each chorus. According to Richard Hill (see no. 386), it "should be used with care, since some of the analyses are incorrect."

—op. 35:6

See no. 293 (Polnauer, Josef. "Schönbergs 'Verbundenheit'" in Arnold Schönberg zum 60. Geburtstag, 1934, p. 44-49).

—op. 50a (Dreimal tausend Jahre)

418   Keller, Hans. "The half-year's new music," Mus rev 15:218-219 (Aug 1954).
Capsule outline of op. 50a and 50b; gives the row of the latter.

—op. 50b (De Profundis)

419   Hill, Richard S. "Music reviews; Arnold Schoenberg: De Profundis," Notes 10:682-683 (Sept 1953).
Row structure.

See no. 418 (Keller, Hans. "The half-year's new music," Aug 1954).

See no. 204a (Rochberg, George. "The harmonic tendency of the hexachord," Nov 1959).

—op. 50c (Moderne Psalmen)

420   Stuckenschmidt, Hans Heinz. "Moderne Psalmen von Arnold Schönberg," ÖMZ 12:47-50 (Feb 1957). Port.
Brief discussion of the text and music.

421   Wörner, Karl H. "'Und trotzdem bete ich': Arnold Schönbergs letztes Werk: 'Moderne Psalmen,'" NZfM 118:147-151 (Mar 1957). Mus., port.
Discussion of the text, with a very brief characterization of the music.

422   Keller, Hans. "The new in review; Schönberg II: the last work," Mus rev 18:221-224 (Aug 1957).
On the origin of the text, and some general comments about the structure.

423   Vlad, Roman. "Moderne Psalmen von Arnold Schönberg," Melos 24:252-255 (Sept 1957). Illus. [facsim. from the autograph MS.].
Discussion of Schoenberg's religious compositions; background

of Moderne Psalmen. Not an analysis, but rather a philosophical critique.

Concerto for piano and orchestra

See no. 388 (Jalowetz, Heinrich. "On the spontaneity of Schoenberg's music," Oct 1944).

424   Leibowitz, René. "Schönbergs Klavierkonzert," Melos 16:44-48 (Feb 1949). Mus.
        Principally a row and thematic analysis.

See no. 368 (Newlin, Dika. "Arnold Schönberg in Amerika," May/June 1952).

Concerto for violin and orchestra

425   Rubin, Louis. The idiom of the violin in twentieth century music. 71 l. Mus. (Thesis, M.A., University of California, Berkeley, 1952).
        On performance technique. Many examples from the Schoenberg Concerto; the Berg Violin concerto and Webern's Four pieces for violin and piano are also discussed.

426   Keller, Hans. "First performances," Mus rev 13:307-309 (Nov 1952).
        Witty review of Schoenberg's Violin concerto and Variations on a recitative for organ.

427   Walters, Willard Gibson. Technical problems in modern violin music as found in selected concertos, with related original exercises and études. [Ann Arbor, Mich., University Microfilms], 1958. 261 l. (Thesis, Ph.D., State University of Iowa.)
        Not seen; abstract in Dissertation Abstracts, v. 18, no. 6, p. 2163. Discusses seven concertos, including Berg's and Schoenberg's.

De Profundis
See his Choral works—op. 50b

Drei Klavierstücke, op. 11
See his Piano works—op. 11

Dreimal tausend Jahre
See his Choral works—op. 50a

Erwartung
See also his Operas

See no. 288 (Bekker, Paul. "Schönberg: 'Erwartung'" in Arnold Schönberg zum fünfzigsten Geburtstag, 1924, p. 275-282.

428   Stefan, Paul. "Schönberg's operas," Modern music 7:24-28 (Dec 1929/Jan 1930).
        On Erwartung and Die glückliche Hand. Reprinted in no. 295 (Armitage), p. 195-204.

429   Craft, Robert. "Schoenberg's Erwartung," Counterpoint 17:13-15
       (Sept 1952).
          Brief discussion of Schoenberg's operas, particularly Erwartung.

430   Dace, Wallace. "The dramatic structure of Schönberg's Erwartung,"
       Educational theater journal [Austin, Texas] 5:322-327 (Dec 1953).
          Erwartung as a psychological melodrama; the dramatic and
       musical techniques used.

                        Fantasy for violin

See no. 300 (Newlin, Dika. "Schoenberg's new Fantasy" in The canon;
       Arnold Schoenberg jubilee issue, Sept 1949).

See no. 400 (Keller, Hans. "Schoenberg," June 1951).

431   Hill, Richard S. "Music reviews; Arnold Schoenberg: Phantasy for
       violin, with piano accompaniment, op. 47," Notes 9:647-648 (Sept
       1952).
          Discusses the hexachordal treatment of the row.

432   Forte, Allen. Contemporary tone structures. New York, Teachers'
       College, Columbia University, 1955. 194 p. Mus.
          An attempt to interpret contemporary musical structure in the
       the light of Heinrich Schenker's analytical theories. Detailed
       row analysis of Schoenberg's Fantasy, p. 110-127, 175-186.

See no. 103 (Gottschalk, Nathan. Twelve note music as developed by
       Arnold Schoenberg, 1956).

                   Five orchestral pieces, op. 16
                     See his Orchestral pieces, op. 16

                   Friede auf Erden
                     See his Choral works—op. 13

                   Fünf Orchesterstücke, op. 16
                     See his Orchestral pieces, op. 16

                   Glückliche Hand
                     See also his Operas

See no. 428 (Stefan, Paul. "Schönberg's operas," Dec 1929/Jan 1930).

433   Keller, Hans. "New music: two Schönberg problems," Mus rev
       17:268-269 (Aug 1956).
          The problems are the meaning of the text and the use of
       Sprechstimme.

434   Keller, Hans. "The 'lucky' hand and other errors," Listener 58:961
       (Dec 5, 1957).
          Corrections of some errors that have been perpetuated in writ-

ings about Schoenberg's opera: the translation of the title, the date of the opera's composition, etc.

Herzgewächse

See no. 74 (Der blaue Reiter, 1914).

Jakobsleiter

See no. 295 (Viertel, Berthold. "Schoenberg's Jakobsleiter" in Armitage, Merle, ed. Schoenberg, 1937, p. 165-181).

See no. 404 (Rankle, Karl. "Arnold Schönberg," May 1952).

435   Zillig, Winfried. "Notes on Arnold Schoenberg's unfinished oratorio, 'Die Jakobsleiter,'" Score, no. 25:7-16 (June 1959). Mus.
      Based on "the entire material connected with the composition of Die Jakobsleiter."

Kammersymphonie, op. 9

436   Berg, Alban. Arnold Schönberg: Kammersymphonie, op. 9. Thematische Analyse. Wien, Universal Edition [192-?] 14 p.
      Thematic form outline; gives measure numbers. No musical examples.

See no. 143 (Schoenberg, Arnold. "Composition with twelve tones" in his Style and idea, 1950).

Kol Nidre

437   Werner, Eric. "Current chronicle: France," MQ 44:242-244 (Apr 1958).
      A description, not an analysis; primarily of the text.

Moderne Psalmen

See his Choral works—op. 50c

Moses und Aron

See also his Operas

438   Bachmann, Claus-Henning. "Ein Wechsel auf die Zukunft," ZfM 115:244-246 (Apr 1954).
      A review of the first performance, with some mention of the row technique and the meaning of the text.

439   Hamel, Fred. "Arnold Schönbergs Bekenntniswerk: zur Uraufführung von Moses und Aron," Musica 8:145-148 (Apr 1954). Illus.
      Background of the opera; its central idea; the first performance.

440   Wörner, Karl H. "Current chronicle: Germany," MQ 40:403-412 (July 1954). Mus.
      Outline of the plot; general description of the music.

441   Rufer, Josef. "Intorno alla genesi del Moses und Aaron di Schoenberg," Aut aut, no. 27:187-195 (May 1955).
      History of the composition of Moses und Aron.

442   Babbitt, Milton. "An introduction to the music" in Moses und Aron
[a booklet issued with Columbia recording K3L-241]. [New York,
Columbia Records, c1957], p. [4-6]. Diagrs.
      A technical analysis of the row structure.

443   Zillig, Winfried. "Schoenbergs Moses und Aron," Melos 24:69-71
(Mar 1957). Illus.
      General article; discussion of the text and the opera as a whole.
      Includes a reproduction of a page of the autograph MS.

444   Reich, Willi. "Ein Briefwechsel über 'Moses und Aron,'" Schw MZ
97:259-260 (June 1957).
      Letters dating from 1930, between Schoenberg and Berg, con-
      cerning Schoenberg's opera.

445   Reich, Willi. "Arnold Schönbergs Oper 'Moses und Aron'; szenische
Uraufführung im Stadttheater Zürich," Schw MZ 97:296-298 (July
1957).
      Sketch of the plot and general description of the music.

446   Rebling, Eberhard. "Arnold Schönbergs Lebensbekenntnis: Gedanken
zu seiner Oper 'Moses und Aron,'" Musik und Gesellschaft [E. Ber-
lin] 7:462-467 (Aug 1957). Illus., port.
      Discussion of the work on philosophical grounds; Moses und Aron
      seen as a sociological commentary.

447   Wörner, Karl H. "Die 39 Schlusstakte von Schönbergs 'Moses und
Aron': Polyphonie der Symbole," Melos 24:350-352 (Dec 1957). Mus.
      "Abschnitt aus einer grösseren Studie des Verfassers." (See
      no. 448a.) Analysis of the closing 39 measures of the opera.

See no. 353 (Keller, Hans. "Moses, Freud, and Schönberg," Jan-Apr 1958).

448   Keller, Hans. "The new in review. Schönberg—III: Moses and Aron,"
Mus rev 19:52-54 (Feb 1958).
      A philosophical discussion of the reasons for the opera's being
      unfinished.

448a Wörner, Karl H. Gotteswort und Magie: die Oper 'Moses und Aron'
von Arnold Schönberg. Heidelberg, Lambert Schneider, 1959. 93 p.
Mus., port.
      Contents: "Das Religiöse in Schönbergs Schaffen," p. 12-18; "'Moses
      und Aron'—die geistige Welt," p. 20-28; "Zur Dialektik der Idee,"
      p. 29-32; "Die musikalischen Grossformen," p. 33-44; "Gott als
      Gedanke," p. 45-55; "Gott als Unendlichkeit," p. 56-58; "Gottes Ver-
      heissung," p. 59-69; "Aron—der ewige Wandel," p. 70-71; "Musik,
      Sprache und Symbole," p. 72-76; "Der dritte Akt," p. 77-78; "Der
      Zwölftoncharacter der Musik," p. 79-87; "Der Aufführungen," p.
      88-91.

−Dance around the golden calf

See no. 811 ([Keller, Hans]. "First performances: Schoenbergians and Stravinskyians," Nov 1954).

Ode to Napoleon

449   List, Kurt. "[Homage to Schönberg]: Ode to Napoleon," Modern music 21:139-145 (Mar/Apr 1944). Mus.
      Discusses many aspects of the work: phrase structure, tonality, motivic treatment, etc.

Operas

See also his Erwartung, Glückliche Hand, Moses und Aron, Von Heute auf Morgen.

450   Felber, Erwin. "Arnold Schönberg und die Oper," Musikblätter des Anbruch 9:67-70 (Jan/Feb 1927).
      Wagner's influence on Schoenberg; discussion of Erwartung, Jakobsleiter, Glückliche Hand.

451   Berg, Alban. "Die Stimme in der Oper," Musikblätter des Anbruch 10:349-350 (Nov/Dec 1928).
      Brief description of the voice treatment in Schoenberg's operas and in Berg's Wozzeck.

452   Leibowitz, René. "Les oeuvres d'Arnold Schoenberg ou la conscience du drame futur dans la musique contemporaine" in Le théâtre musical. Paris, Richard-Masse [1947/48], p. 84-104. Mus. (Polyphonie, 1er cahier).
      Erwartung (one of the few articles discussing its construction), Glückliche Hand, Von Heute auf Morgen, and (briefly) Moses und Aron.

453   Mayer, Harry. "Twee toneelwerken van Arnold Schoenberg," Mens en melodie 13:135-139 (May 1958). Mus.
      Erwartung and Von Heute auf Morgen; a brief account of the music and the drama.

454   Mitchell, Donald. "Summer festivals: Von Heute auf Morgen and Erwartung," Opera [London] 9:567-571 (Sept 1958). Illus.
      Brief review and general description.

Orchestral pieces, op. 16

See no. 307 (Newman, Ernest. "A propos of Schönberg's five orchestral pieces," Feb 1, 1914).

455   Deutsch, Max. "Les cinq Pièces pour Orchestre d'Arnold Schön-berg," Schw MZ 88:462-464 (Dec 1948).
      "Conférence donnée à Radio-Genève."
      A somewhat philosophical discussion; not an analysis.

456   Cowell, Henry. "Current chronicle: New York," MQ 35:106-111 (Jan
      1949). Mus.
      A review and description of Schoenberg's Five orchestral pieces
      and Webern's Passacaglia.

See no. 306a (Adorno, Theodor Wiesengrund. "Zur Vorgeschichte der
      Reihenkomposition" in his Klangfiguren, 1959).

                  Orchestral variations, op. 31

            See his Variations for orchestra, op. 31

            Phantasy for violin

            See his Fantasy for violin

            Piano works

457   Deutsch, Leonhard. "Zur Einführung in die Harmonik der zeitge-
      nössischen Klavierliteratur," Musikblätter des Anbruch 9:324-34 .
      (Oct/Nov 1927). Mus.
      "Zwölftontechnik (Schönberg)," p. 339-342.
      Discusses briefly the Three pieces, op. 11; Six little pieces,
      op. 19; Five pieces, op. 23.

See no. 295 (Steuermann, Eduard. "The piano music of Schoenberg" in
      Armitage, Merle, ed. Schoenberg, 1937, p. 125-133).

458   Tuttle, T. Temple. "Schönberg's compositions for piano solo," Mus
      rev 18:300-318 (Nov 1957). Mus.
      Analyses of op. 11, 19, 23, 33a, 33b. Seems to rely on previous
      analyses by Leibowitz and Dika Newlin.

                  —op. 11 (Three piano pieces)

See no. 380 (Somigli, Carlo. "Il modus operandi di Arnold Schoenberg,"
      [Jul/Sept] 1913).

See no. 389 (Katz, Adele T. Challenge to musical tradition, 1945).

459   Leichtentritt, Hugo. "Arnold Schönberg: opus 11 and opus 19" in
      his Musical form. Cambridge, Harvard University Press, 1951,
      p. 425-450. Mus.
      "The present attempt at analysis . . . is concerned with whether
      it is possible to discover a rational constructive idea in these
      pieces . . ."
      The analysis of op. 19 appeared originally in Modern music,
      May/June 1928.

                  —op. 11:1

460   Koperberg-Van Wermeskerken, A. "Bij een pianostuk van Schoen-
      berg," Mens en melodie 7:382-384 (Dec 1952). Mus.
      Brief analysis of the variation technique.

—op. 19 (Six little piano pieces)

See no. 459 (Leichtentritt, Hugo. "Arnold Schönberg: opus 11 and opus 19" in his Musical form, 1951).

See no. 586 (Pousseur, Henri. "Da Schoenberg a Webern," Dec 1956).

—op. 19:2

See no. 159 (Ballif, Claude. Introduction à la métatonalité, 1956, p. 111).

—op. 25 (Suite for piano)

See no. 384 (Westphal, Kurt. Arnold Schönbergs Weg zur Zwölftonmusik," Apr 1929).

See no. 389 (Katz, Adele T. Challenge to musical tradition, 1945).

See no. 143 (Schoenberg, Arnold. "Composition with twelve tones" in his Style and idea, 1950).

—op. 33a

See no. 28 ([Keller, Hans]. "First performances and their reviews," Feb 1953).

See no. 155 (Ogdon, Wilbur Lee. Series and structure, 1955, p. 28-92).

461   Mayer, Harry. "Een blik achter de werkwijze van Arnold Schoenberg," Mens en melodie 12:130-133 (May 1957). Mus., port.
      Analysis of the row treatment.

Pieces for orchestra, five

See his Orchestral pieces, op. 16

Pierrot Lunaire, op. 21

462   Godet, Robert. "Après une audition de 'Pierrot Lunaire,'" Rev mus 7:19-30 (May 1923).
      Impressions of the work; not an analysis.

463   Engel, Carl. "Schönberg Lunaire" in his Dischords mingled. New York, Knopf, 1931, p. 84-97.
      A nontechnical essay.

464   Boulez, Pierre. "Trajectories: Ravel, Stravinsky, Schoenberg," Contrepoints 6:122-142 (1949).
      Discusses one work each by Ravel, Stravinsky, and Schoenberg (see no. 465).

465   Schaeffner, André. "Chroniques et commentaires; variations Schoenberg," Contrepoints 7:110-129 (1951).
      A commentary on Boulez's article (see no. 464).

See no. 303 (Stein, Erwin. "The treatment of the speaking voice in Pierrot Lunaire" in his Orpheus in new guises, 1953, p. 86-89).

See no. 69 (Perle, George. "Theory and practice in twelve-tone music," Jun 1959).

Quartets, Strings

466   Gradenwitz, Peter. "The idiom and development in Schoenberg's quartets," M & L 26:123-142 (Jul 1945). Mus.
       Brief analyses. Includes a list of Schoenberg's works, p. 141-142.

—no. 1, in D minor, op. 7

467   Wellesz, Egon. "Arnold Schönberg," Zeitschrift der Internationalen Musikgesellschaft 12:342-348 (Sept 1911). Mus.
       Discussion of Schoenberg's early works, with outlines of the form of the first and second quartets.

468   Schindler, Kurt. Arnold Schönberg's Quartet in D minor, op. 7: an introductory note . . . delivered . . . at the private performance by the Flonzaley Quartet . . . New York, December 28th, 1913. Followed by an index of musical themes. New York, G. Schirmer [c1914]. 10 p. + 5 p. of "index of themes."

469   "A Schönberg quartet," Musical courier 68:27 (Feb 4, 1914). Port.
       A sympathetic contemporary criticism; discusses the "style" of the work.

470   Berg, Alban. "Why is Schoenberg's music so hard to understand?" Mus rev 13:187-196 (Aug 1952), tr. by Anton Swarowsky and Joseph Lederer.
       Originally appeared as "Warum ist Schönbergs Musik so schwer verständlich?" in Arnold Schönberg zum fünfzigsten Geburtstag (see no. 288), reprinted in Reich's Alban Berg (see no. 402, p. 142-155). French translation—"Pourquoi la musique de Schoenberg est-elle si difficile a comprendre?"—in Berg's Ecrits (see no. 509, p. 65-92).

—no. 2, in F-sharp minor, op. 10

See no. 467 (Wellesz, Egon. "Arnold Schönberg," Sept 1911).

See no. 380 (Somigli, Carlo. "Il modus operandi di Arnold Schoenberg," Jul/Sept 1913).

—no. 3, op. 30

471   Stein, Erwin. "Schönberg's new structural form," Modern music 7:3-10 (Jun/Jul 1930). Mus., port.
       Primarily a row analysis.

See no. 586 (Pousseur, Henri. "Da Schoenberg a Webern," Dec 1956).

—no. 4, op. 37

472   Mangeot, André. "Schoenberg's fourth Quartet," Mus rev 3:33-37 (Feb 1942). Mus.
A brief thematic analysis.

See no. 206 (Johnson, Martha. A study of linear design in Gregorian chant and music written in the twelve-tone technique, 1954).

See no. 166a (Rufer, Josef. "Was ist Zwölftonmusik?" Jan 1958).

—first movement

473   Neighbor, Oliver. "A talk on Schoenberg for Composers' Concourse," Score, no. 16:19-28 (Jun 1956). Mus.
An analysis of the first movement.

Quintet, Winds, op. 26

474   Greissle, Felix. "Die formalen Grundlagen des Bläserquintetts von Arnold Schönberg," Musikblätter des Anbruch 7:63-68 (Feb 1925). Mus.
A brief structural analysis.

475   Pannain, Guido. "L'Internationale Musikgesellschaft für neue Musik e il Festivale musicale di Zurigo; 2° Concerto Schoenberg," Riv mus ital 33:417-421 ([Jul/Sept] 1926).
Brief description of the twelve-tone technique; characteristics of the Quintet.

See no. 384 (Westphal, Kurt. "Arnold Schönbergs Weg zur Zwölftonmusik," Apr 1929).

See no. 143 (Schoenberg, Arnold. "Composition with twelve tones" in his Style and idea, 1950, p. 102-143).

Satires for mixed chorus

See his Choral works—op. 28
(Three satires for mixed chorus)

Sechs kleine Klavierstücke, op. 19

See his Piano works—op. 19

Septet, op. 29

See his Suite (Septet), op. 29

Six little piano pieces, op. 19

See his Piano works—op. 19

Songs

476 Zeiger, Jean Wilson. Early expressionistic songs. (Thesis, M. A.,
     University of California, 1959). 188 l. Mus.
     Bibliography, p. 179-188. Covers songs of Schoenberg, Berg,
     and Webern "written in a non-tonal idiom prior to Schoenberg's
     development of the twelve-tone method." Detailed analyses of
     Schoenberg's op. 15, nos. 4 and 9, Webern's op. 4, no. 2, and
     Webern's op. 15, no. 4.

—op. 6 (Eight songs)

See no. 380 (Somigli, Carlo. "Il modus operandi di Arnold Schoenberg,"
     Jul/Sept 1913).

—op. 15 (Das Buch der hängenden Gärten)

See no. 476 (Zeiger, Jean Wilson. Early expressionistic songs, 1959).

String quartets
   See his Quartets, Strings

String trio
   See his Trio, Strings

Suite, Piano, op. 25
   See his Piano works—op. 25

Suite (Septet), op. 29

477 Stein, Erwin. "Zu Schönbergs neuer Suite, op. 29," Musikblätter
     des Anbruch 9:280-281 (Aug/Sept 1927).
     A brief description.

Survivor from Warsaw

478 Leibowitz, René. "Arnold Schoenberg's 'Survivor from Warsaw' or
     the possibility of 'committed' art," Horizon [London] 20:122-131
     (Aug 1949).
     A philosophical discussion of the political questions involved;
     brief summary of the "plot" and some general statements about
     the music. [Summarized by Paul Hamburger in Mus sur 2:183
     (Winter 1950).]

479 Hill, Richard S. "Music reviews; Arnold Schoenberg: A survivor
     from Warsaw," Notes 7:133-135 (Dec 1949).
     Discusses the row treatment.

See no. 400 (Keller, Hans. "Schoenberg," Jun 1951).

Theme and variations in G minor for orchestra, op. 43b

480   Goehr, Walter. "Musica-Umschau: Schönbergs Aussöhnung mit der
Tonalität," Musica 1:219-220 (May/Aug 1947).
Surveys Schoenberg's various "periods" of composition and
briefly describes these tonal variations.

Trio, Strings, op. 45

481   Hymanson, William. "Schoenberg's String trio (1946)," Mus rev
11:184-194 (Aug 1950). Mus., tables.
The work as a whole; its row treatment.

482   Hill, Richard S. "Music reviews: Arnold Schoenberg: String trio,
op. 45," Notes 8:127-129 (Dec 1950).
Hexachordal row treatment discussed at some length.

483   Neighbor, Oliver W. "Dodecaphony in Schoenberg's String trio,"
Mus sur 4:489-490 (Jun 1952). Mus.
Very brief account of the row treatment.

See no. 204a (Rochberg, George. "The harmonic tendency of the hexachord," Nov 1959).

Variations for orchestra, op. 31

484   Leibowitz, René. Introduction à la musique de douze sons. Les
Variations pour orchestre, op. 31, d'Arnold Schoenberg. Paris,
L'Arche [1949]. 351 p. Mus.
Partial contents: Première partie: "Nécessités et genèse de la
technique de douze sons," p. 25-52; "La 'Reihenkomposition'
antérieure à la technique de douze sons," p. 53-80; "La technique
de douze sons," p. 81-108. Deuxième partie: "Les Variations
pour orchestre," p. 113-220. Troisième partie: "Les dernières
oeuvres de Schoenberg, de Webern et de Berg," p. 223-249;
"Les nouvelles générations de compositeurs 'dodécaphonistes'
et leurs caractéristiques générales," p. 250-276; "Les survivances
de l'ordre tonal à l'intérieur de la technique de douze sons et
les possibilités de leur dépassement," p. 279-302; "Les aspects
les plus récents de la technique de douze sons," p. 303-335;
"Oeuvres d'Arnold Schoenberg," p. 339-342; "Oeuvres d'Alban
Berg," p. 342-343; "Oeuvres d'Anton Webern," p. 343-345.

See no. 143 (Schoenberg, Arnold. "Composition with twelve tones" in his
Style and idea, 1950, p. 102-143).

485   Kloppenburg, W. C. M. "Het thema van Schoenbergs Variationen
Für Orchester," Mens en melodie 12:362-365 (Dec 1957). Mus.
An analysis of the theme.

See no. 170 (Nono, Luigi. "Die Entwicklung der Reihentechnik" in Steinecke, Wolfgang, ed. Darmstädter Beiträge zur neuen Musik, 1958,
p. 25-37).

485a Schoenberg, Arnold. "The orchestral variations, op. 31: a radio
     talk," Score, no. 27:27-40 (Jul 1960). Mus.
          An analysis; originally given over the Frankfurt radio in 1931.

Variations on a recitative for organ, op. 40

See no. 426 (Keller, Hans. "First performances," Nov 1952).

486 Keller, Hans. "First performances: their pre- and reviews," Mus
     rev 16:145-147 (May 1955).
          Discusses "tonality and harmony," "counterpoint," "melody and
          rhythmic structure" very briefly.

Von Heute auf Morgen
See also his Operas

487 Adorno, Theodor Wiesengrund. "Arnold Schönberg: Von Heute auf
     Morgen," Anbruch 13:72-74 (Feb 1930).
          A brief description.

488 Pisk, Paul. "Schoenberg's twelve-tone opera," Modern music 7:18-
     21 (Apr/May 1930).
          Discusses the plot and musical structure. Reprinted in no. 295
          (Armitage).

489 Reich, Willi. "Berichte aus dem Ausland: Schönberg-Premier nach
     22 Jahren," Melos 20:27-28 (Jan 1953). Illus.
          General description of the work and of its first performance
          since 1930.

490 Keller, Hans. "Schoenberg's comic opera," Score, no. 23:27-36 (Jul
     1958).
          A discussion of its history, bibliography, libretto, and music.

Wind quintet, op. 26
See his Quintet, Winds, op. 26

ALBAN BERG (1885-1935)

GENERAL
(Including Collections, Festschriften, etc.)

491 Mantelli, Alberto. "Note su Alban Berg," Rass mus 9:117-132 (Apr
     1936). Mus.
          Berg's works, especially Wozzeck, and his significance.

492 Reich, Willi, ed. Alban Berg: mit Bergs eigenem Schriften und
     Beiträgen von Theodor Wiesengrund Adorno und Ernst Krenek.

Wien, Herbert Reichner [c1937]. 208 p. Mus., ports.
Contents: Biography, p. 7-18; analyses of Berg's works, by Reich,
Adorno, and Krenek, p. 19-133; essays by Berg, p. 135-203.

See no. 81 (Hijman, Julius. Nieuwe oostenrijkse musiek, 1938).

493   Reich, Willi. "Alban Berg" in Thompson, Oscar, ed. Great modern
        composers. New York, Dodd Mead, 1941, p. 10-14.
        Includes a short catalog of Berg's works, p. 14.

See no. 82 (Salazar, Adolfo. Music in our time, 1946).

494   Hübner, Herbert. "Berg, Alban" in Die Musik in Geschichte und
        Gegenwart. Kassel, Bärenreiter, 1949-1951, v. 1, col. 1680-1684.
        Illus.
        Bibliography and list of works included.

See no. 84 (Leibowitz, René. "Alban Berg: the awareness of the past in
        contemporary music" in his Schoenberg and his school, 1949, p.
        137-186).

See no. 299 (Wörner, Karl H. Music der Gegenwart, 1949).

495   Reich, Willi. "Berg, Alban" in Grove's Dictionary of music and
        musicians. 5th ed., London, Macmillan, 1954, v. 1, p. 635-639.
        Includes a list of works and a bibliography.

See no. 94 (Rognoni, Luigi. Espressionismo e dodecafonia, 1954).

See no. 100 (Collaer, Paul. La musique moderne, 1905-1955, 1955).

See no. 105 (Hamilton, Iain. "Alban Berg and Anton Webern" in Hartog,
        Howard, ed. European music in the twentieth century, 1957, p.
        94-117).

496   Redlich, Hans Ferdinand. Alban Berg, the man and his music.
        New York, Abelard-Schuman [c1957]. 316 p. Mus., ports.

        _____. Alban Berg: Versuch einer Würdigung. Wien, Universal
        Edition, 1957.
        Contents: Part 1: "The second Viennese school," p. 13-18; "The
        problem of tonality," p. 19-31. Part 2: "The music of Alban
        Berg," p. 35-202. Part 3: "The life of Alban Berg," p. 217-242.
        Part 4: appendices: "Arnold Schoenberg on Alban Berg" (1949),
        p. 245-246; "Facsimile of Berg's Variations for piano on a theme
        of his own" (1908), p. 247-259; "Berg's lecture on Wozzeck"
        (1929), p. 261-285; "Catalogue of works," p. 287-298; "Discog-
        raphy," p. 299-304; "Bibliography," p. 305-312.
        Review by Ernst Krenek in MQ 43:403-406 (July 1957).

See no. 112 (Prieberg, Fred K. Lexikon der neuen Musik, 1958, p. 36-41).

See no. 115 (Stuckenschmidt, Hans Heinz. "Alban Berg" in his Schöpfer
        der neuen Musik, 1958, p. 180-191).

See no. 116 (Vlad, Roman. "Berg e la libera articolazione della dodeca-
        fonia" in his Storia della dodecafonia, 1958, p. 115-124).

497 Adorno, Theodor Wiesengrund. "Alban Berg" in his Klangfiguren. Berlin, Suhrkamp Verlag, c1959, p. 121-137. (His Musikalischen Schriften, I.)
   "Ursprünglich ein Vortrag für den Norddeutschen Rundfunk, veröffentlich in 'Merkur,' 10. Jahrgang, Heft 7, Juli 1956, S. 643 ff."

498 Vogelsang, Konrad. Alban Berg, Leben und Werk. Berlin-Halensee, Max Hesses Verlag [c1959]. 88 p. Ports. (Hesses kleine Bücherei, Band 5.)
   Contents: Part 1: "Leben," p. 9-54. Part 2: "Werkanalysen," p. 55-77; "Werkverzeichnis," p. 79-81; "Discographie," p. 81-85; "Bibliographie," p. 86-88.

See no. 118a (Zillig, Winifried. "Alban Berg und die Wiener Schule" in his Variationen über neue Musik, 1959, p. 140-148).

498a Boulez, Pierre. "Alban Berg heute gesehen," Melos 27:33-36 (Feb 1960).
   Exerpted from his article in Fasquelle's Encyclopèdie de la musique [c1958]; tr. by Pierre Stoll.

PHILOSOPHY AND CRITICISM

499 Pijper, Willem. "Alban Berg," MT 77:414-415 (May 1936), tr. by Herbert Antcliffe.
   Obituary; general evaluation of Berg's work. The author feels that, with Berg's death, the "period of atonal composition is for the time being already concluded."

500 Holländer, Hans. "Alban Berg," MQ 22:375-382 (Oct 1936), tr. by "G. R." Port.
   General essay on the importance of Berg.

501 Menasce, Jacques. "Berg and Bartók," Modern music 21:76-81 (Jan/Feb 1944).
   Affinities between the two composers.

502 Leibowitz, René. "Innovation and tradition in contemporary music: III. Alban Berg, or the seduction to truth," Horizon [London] 16: 140-152 (Aug 1947).
   Conclusion of his series of articles on Schoenberg, Webern, and Berg (see nos. 320 and 575).

503 Boulez, Pierre. "Incidences actuelles de Berg; à propos de la Quinzaine de Musique autrichienne à Paris" in Le rythme musical. Paris, Richard-Masse [1948], p. 104-108. Mus. (Polyphonie, 2e cahier.)
   Berg's relation to musical tradition.

See no. 29 (Goléa, Antoine. "Alban Berg" in his Esthétique de la musique contemporaine, 1954, p. 52-56, 66-71).

504   Lindlar, Heinrich. "'Mir fehlt die grosse Freude'; zum 20. Todes-
      tag Alban Bergs," Musica 9:594-596 (Dec 1955). Illus.
      An evaluation of Berg's works twenty years after his death.

505   Rubin, Marcel. "Alban Berg und die Zukunft der Schönberg-Schule,"
      Musik und Gesellschaft [E. Berlin] 5:384-386 (Dec 1955). Mus.
      Feels that Berg's works, having tonal implications, could more
      practically have been written within a tonal idiom. Finds Berg
      the only twelve-tone composer who appeals to the masses, and
      therefore the one by which the trend of dodecaphony should be
      judged. Discusses folk elements in Wozzeck.

                              BIOGRAPHY

506   Reich, Willi. "Erinnerungen an Alban Berg," Schw MZ 91:1-3 (Jan
      1951).
      "Gesprochen im Südwestfunk in Baden-Baden im Dezember 1950."

507   Schmidt-Garre, Helmut. "Berg als Lehrer," Melos 22:40-41 (Feb
      1955). Illus.
      A brief comment by a former Berg pupil.

508   Reich, Willi. "Alban Berg als Apologet Arnold Schönbergs: mit
      einem unbekannten Aufsatz Bergs," Schw MZ 95:475-477 (Dec 1955).
      Gives the first part of an article by Berg. (The second part of
      Berg's article was previously published as "Zwei Feuilletons:
      Ein Beitrag zum Kapitel, 'Schönberg und die Kritik'" in the
      Neuer Wiener Journal, July 17, 1920).

509   Berg, Alban. Ecrits: choisis, traduits, et commentés par Henri
      Pousseur. Monaco, Editions du Rocher [1957]. 182 p. Mus.
      (Domaine musical.)
      Partial contents: "La société viennoise d'exécutions privées"
      (1919), p. 29-37; "Pourquoi la musique de Schoenberg est-elle
      si difficile à comprendre?" (1924), p. 65-92; "Lettre ouverte à
      Schoenberg" (1925), p. 93-108; "A propos des formes employées
      dans Wozzeck" (1924), p. 109-117; "Indications pratiques pour
      l'étude de Wozzeck" (1930), p. 141-155; "Credo" (1930), p. 157-
      166; "Chronologie," p. 167-178.

*509a Reich, Willi, ed. Alban Berg, Bildnis im Wort: Selbstzeugnisse
      und Aussagen der Freunde. Zürich, Die Arche [c1959]. 89 p.
      Illus., mus., ports.

510   Schoenberg, Arnold. "Über Alban Berg," Schw MZ 99:221-225 (Jun
      1959).
      Originally written for Reich's book on Berg (see no. 492).

CORRESPONDENCE

See no. 374 (Hill, Richard S. "Annual reports on acquisitions: music,"
Nov 1952).

511   Reich, Willi. "Aus unbekannten Briefen von Alban Berg an Anton
Webern: Alban Berg als Opernkomponist und Musikschriftsteller,"
Schw MZ 93:49-52 (Feb 1953).
Brief note concerning the friendship between Berg and Webern;
texts of five letters.

See no. 555 (Blaukopf, Kurt. "New light on Wozzeck," Sept 26, 1953).

512   Redlich, Hans Ferdinand. "Alle guten Dinge," Melos 22:39-40 (Feb
1955).
Excerpts from letters of Berg to Schoenberg and Webern concerning Berg's Chamber concerto. Reprinted in Redlich's Alban
Berg (see no. 496).

513   Reich, Willi. "Aus Alban Bergs Jugendzeit," Melos 22.33-38 (Feb
1955). Port.
The young Berg; selections from early letters.

514   Rufer, Josef. "Dokumente einer Freundschaft," Melos 22:42-46 (Feb
1955). Illus., port.
Letters from Berg to Schoenberg.

See no. 444 (Reich, Willi. "Ein Briefwechsel über 'Moses und Aron,'"
Jun 1957).

See no. 379 ([Schoenberg, Arnold]. "Ein unbekannter Brief von Arnold
Schönberg an Alban Berg," Jan 1959).

COMPOSITIONAL TECHNIQUES

See no. 391 (Wood, Ralph W. "Concerning 'Sprechgesang,'" Dec 1946).

See no. 154 (Erickson, Robert. The structure of music, 1955).

See no. 160 (Perle, George. Serial composition and atonality, 1956 [c1959].)

GENERAL DESCRIPTIONS OF WORKS

See no. 292 (Mersmann, Hans. Die moderne Musik seit der Romantik,
1927).

515   Reich, Willi. "Alban Berg," Die Musik 22:347-353 (Feb 1930). Mus.,
port.
A discussion of Berg's works and "style." Includes the complete
music of Berg's two settings of "Schliesse mir die Augen beide,"
made in 1900 and 1925.

516   Adorno, Theodor Wiesengrund. "Berg and Webern—Schoenberg's heirs," Modern music 8:29-38 (Jan 1931).
       Discussion and comparison of Berg's and Webern's works and "styles."

517   Reich, Willi. "Les dernières oeuvres d'Alban Berg," Rev mus 12:148-154 (Feb 1931).
       A brief discussion.

518   Mantelli, Alberto. "Elenco delle opere di Berg," Rass mus 9:163-164 (May 1936).
       A list of Berg's works.

See no. 492 (Reich, Willi, ed. Alban Berg, 1937, p. 19-133).

See no. 484 (Leibowitz, René. "Les dernières oeuvres de Schoenberg, de Webern et de Berg" in his Introduction à la musique de douze sons, 1949, p. 223-249).

See no. 403 (Demuth, Norman. "Alban Berg" in his Musical trends in the twentieth century, 1952, p. 239-245).

519   "Oeuvres d'Alban Berg (1885-1935)," Music information record, no. 11:15, 17 (Winter 1953/1954).
       List of works with dates of publication.

See no. 95 (Wörner, Karl H. Neue Musik in der Entscheidung, 1954).

INDIVIDUAL WORKS

Altenberger Lieder
See his Songs—op. 4

Chamber concerto for violin, piano, and 13 winds

520   Deutsch, Max. "Le Concerto de chambre d'Alban Berg," Schw MZ 89:328-333 (Sept 1949).
       The background of the work, its symbolism, its general characteristics.

See no. 94 (Berg, Alban. "Lettera aperta ad Arnold Schoenberg" in Rognoni, Luigi. Espressionismo e dodecafonia, 1954, p. 277-282).
       Originally published in Pult und Taktstock, 1925.

See no. 512 (Redlich, Hans Ferdinand. "Alle guten Dinge," Feb 1955).

Concerto, Violin and orchestra

521   Smith, Moses. "Alban Berg—finale: a requiem," Modern music 13:29-34 (Mar 1936). Port.
       Some comments on Lulu, but primarily an essay on the Violin concerto: its genesis and character.

522   Carner, Mosco. "Alban Berg (1885-1935)" in Hill, Ralph. The con-
      certo. London, Penguin Books, 1952, p. 362-379. Mus.
         An extended but nontechnical analysis.

See no. 425 (Rubin, Louis. The idiom of the violin in twentieth century
      music, 1952).

See no. 649 (Gavazzeni, Gianandrea. "La critica soggettivistica e il Con-
      certo per violino di Berg" in his Musicisti d'Europa, 1954, p. 124-
      129).

523   Rostal, Max, and Hans Keller. "Berg's Violin concerto: a revision,"
      MT 95:87-88 (Feb 1954). Mus.
         Problems of alternate versions of the cadenza in the second
      movement.

524   Redlich, Hans Ferdinand. "Alban Bergs Violinkonzert," Melos 24:
      316-321 (Nov 1957) and 24:352-357 (Dec 1957). Mus.
         An analysis. Reprinted from Redlich's Alban Berg (see no. 496).

See no. 427 (Walters, Willard Gibson. Technical problems in modern
      violin music, 1958).

Five songs to postcard texts
See his Songs—op. 4

Kammerkonzert
See his Chamber concerto

Lulu
See also his Operas

525   Collaer, Paul. "Une nouvelle oeuvre d'Alban Berg: Loulou," Rev
      mus 16:169-174 (Mar 1934). Mus.
         The structure of the drama and the music; a survey-analysis.

526   Bach, David Joseph. "New music by Berg, Webern, Krenek,"
      Modern music 12:31-38 (Nov/Dec 1934).
         A review of the music (Berg's Lulu, Webern's Songs, op. 23,
      and Krenek's Cantata, op. 72) and a summary of the trends of
      twelve-tone music in the mid-1930's.

527   Reich, Willi. "Lulu, the text and music," Modern music 12:103-111
      (Mar/Apr 1935). Port.
         A summary of the drama and a brief general discussion of the
      music.

528   Reich, Willi. "Alban Berg's Lulu," MQ 22:383-401 (Oct 1936), tr.
      by M. D. Herter Norton. Mus.
         The dramatic and musical structure of the opera.

529   List, Kurt. "Lulu, after the première," Modern music 15:8-12
      (Nov/Dec 1937).

A general summation of Berg's achievements; a review of Lulu—the performance and the music.

530 Thoresby, Christina. "Lulu d'Alban Berg au théâtre," Contrepoints 6:156-159 (1949). Mus.
Brief summary of the plot and the musical technique.

531 Reich, Willi. "Deutsche Première nach 15 Jahren: Alban Bergs Oper 'Lulu,'" Melos 19:337-342 (Dec 1952). Illus., port.
Background of the opera; outline of the plot.

532 Hill, Richard S. "Reviews of records; Berg: Lulu," MQ 39:134-138 (Jan 1953).
Comparison of Lulu with Wozzeck and Schoenberg's Erwartung; the origin of the text of Lulu; the character of the music.

533 Werker, Gerard. "Alban Berg en zijn opera Lulu," Mens en melodie 8:167-172 (Jun 1953). Mus., port.
Some row analysis; a sketch of the drama.

534 Mitchell, Donald. "The character of Lulu: Wedekind's and Berg's conceptions compared," Mus rev 15:268-274 (Nov 1954). Mus.
Berg and Wedekind as librettists; Berg's musical treatment of the drama.

535 Krenek, Ernst. "Alban Bergs 'Lulu'" in his Zur Sprache Gebracht: Essays über Musik. München, Albert Langen [c1958], p. 241-250.
Reprinted from the Wiener Zeitung, June 6, 1937.

See no. 69 (Perle, George. "Theory and practice in twelve-tone music," Jun 1959).

Lulu Symphonie

535a Adorno, Theodor Wiesengrund. "Bergs Lulu-Symphonie," Melos 27:43-46 (Feb 1960).
Reprinted from the fall 1935 issue of 23, eine Wiener Musikzeitschrift.

535b Reich, Willi. "An der Seite von Alban Berg," Melos 27:36-42 (Feb 1960). Mus.
Includes facsimiles of three sketches for Lulu.

Lyric suite for string quartet

536 Bouquet, Fritz. "Alban Bergs 'Lyrische Suite'; eine Studie über Gestalt, Klang und Ausdruck," Melos 15:227-231 (Aug/Sept 1948). Mus.
Analysis, especially of the row treatment and the form.

See no. 144 (Brainard, Paul. "Lyric suite" in his A study of the twelve-tone technique, 1951, p. 34-58).

537 Smith Brindle, Reginald. "The symbolism in Berg's 'Lyric suite,'" Score, no. 21:60-63 (Oct 1957). Mus.
A deciphering of Berg's musical symbolism.

See no. 69 (Perle, George. "Theory and practice in twelve-tone music,"
    Jun 1959).

Operas
See also his Lulu, Wozzeck

538 Leibowitz, René. "Alban Berg et l'essence de l'opéra," L'arche
     [pt. 1] "Réflexions sur la musique dramatique sub una specie,"
     no. 13:130-134 (Feb 1946); [pt. 2] "Problèmes et architecture des
     opéras de Berg," no. 14:158-166 (Mar 1946).
         Berg and the problems of opera.

539 Grout, Donald Jay. "Opera between two wars" in his A short his-
     tory of opera. One-volume ed. New York, Columbia University
     Press [c1947], p. 532-535. Mus.
         Brief outline of the dramatic and musical structure of Wozzeck
         and Lulu. Bibliographical notes.

Schliesse mir die Augen beide
See his Songs—Schliesse mir die Augen beide

Songs

540 Adorno, Theodor Wiesengrund. "Die Instrumentation von Bergs
     frühen Liedern" in his Klangfiguren. Berlin, Suhrkamp Verlag,
     c1959, p. 138-156. (His Musikalischen Schriften, I.)
         Originally published in Schweizerische Musikzeitschrift und
         Sängerblatt, 5/6:158 ff., 198 ff. (Mar 1932). Revised.

See no. 476 (Zeiger, Jean Wilson. Early expressionistic songs, 1959).

—op. 2, no. 4

See no. 74 (Der blaue Reiter, 1914).

—op. 4
(Five songs to postcard texts by Peter Altenberg)

541 Leibowitz, René. "Alban Berg's Five orchestral songs, after post-
     card texts by Peter Altenberg, op. 4," MQ 34:487-511 (Oct 1948).
     Mus., port.
         "A brief survey of the essential elements of the first four songs
         and a complete analysis of the last song" (the music of which is
         reproduced in a piano reduction).

542 Ringger, Rolf Urs. "Zur formbildenden Kraft des vertonten Wortes:
     analytische Untersuchen an Liedern von Hugo Wolf und Alban Berg,"
     Schw MZ 99:225-229 (Jun 1959). Mus.
         A comparison of Wolf's "Das verlassene Mägdlein" (Mörikelieder)
         and Berg's op. 4 songs. The score of op. 4, no. 2, is given com-
         plete.

—Schliesse mir die Augen beide

See no. 515 (Reich, Willi. "Alban Berg," Feb 1930).

—Der Wein

See his Der Wein

Variations for piano

See no. 496 (Redlich, Hans Ferdinand. Alban Berg, 1957, p. 247-259).

Violin concerto

See his Concerto, Violin and orchestra

Der Wein

543   Reich, Willi. "Berg's new work, 'Der Wein,'" Modern music 7:41-
43 (Apr/May 1930).
A description; the row is quoted.

Wozzeck

See also his Operas

544   Viebig, Ernst. "Bergs 'Wozzeck': ein Beitrag zum Opernproblem,"
Die Musik 15:506-510 (Apr 1923).
The background of the opera; the text, the musical forms used;
its place in operatic tradition.

545   Alban Bergs 'Wozzeck' und die Musikkritik. Herausgeber: Musikblätter des Anbruch. Wien [1925?]. 31 p. Mus. (Musik der Gegenwart; eine Flugblätterfolge, nr. 9.)
Contemporary reviews of Berg's opera; some analyses.

546   Winkler, Hans. Georg Büchners "Woyzeck." Greifswald, E. Hart-
mann, 1925. 238 p.
An analysis of Büchner's drama (not of Berg's opera); bibliography, p. 235-236.

547   Adorno, Theodor Wiesengrund. "Alban Berg: zur Uraufführung des
'Wozzeck,'" Musikblätter des Anbruch 7:531-537 (Dec 1925).
General comments on the first performance.

548   Reich, Willi. Alban Berg's Wozzeck; a guide to the text and music
of the opera. New York, G. Schirmer [c1927]. 22 p. Mus., port.
"Reprinted from the monograph originally published by the League
of Composers' Quarterly Review, Modern Music."
Contents: "Synopsis of the opera," p. 1-2; "Berg's organization of
the text," p. 2-4; "The musical structure as a whole," p. 4-6;
"Scheme of the dramatic and musical forms," p. 7; "Analysis of
the individual scenes," p. 8-21; "Postscript by Alban Berg," p.
21-22.

See no. 451 (Berg, Alban. "Die Stimme in der Oper," Nov/Dec 1928).

549   Sabin, Robert. "Alban Berg's Wozzeck," Musical America 71:6-7,
      34 (Apr 1, 1951). Illus.
         Fritz Mahler's analytical charts are explained. (Fritz Mahler
         was a pupil of Berg.) (See no. 561.)

550   Keller, Hans. "First performances: the eclecticism of Wozzeck,"
      Mus rev 12:309-315 (Nov 1951) and 13:133-137 (May 1952). Mus.

551   Gerhard, Roberto. "Wozzeck," Foyer [London], no. 2:16-20 (Winter,
      1951/52). Mus., port.
         A brief outline of the plot and the musical structure.

552   Berg, Alban. "The musical form in Wozzeck," Opera [London]
      3:23-24 (Jan 1952), tr by Erwin Stein. Illus.
         Originally published as "Das Opernproblem" in the Neue Musik-
         zeitung [Stuttgart] 49:285 ff. (Nov 1928).
         A brief article stating that Berg's various "closed forms" are
         used in Wozzeck for compactness but are not to be perceived
         by the audience as such.

553   Stein, Erwin. "Wozzeck," Opera [London] 3:17-22 (Jan 1952). Illus.
         History of Wozzeck; its performances and general characteris-
         tics; the drama and a few comments on the music. Reprinted
         in Stein's Orpheus in new guises, p. 103-107 (see no. 303).

554   Jouve, Pierre Jean. Wozzeck ou le nouvel opéra, [par] Pierre-
      Jean Jouve [et] Michel Fano. Paris, Plon [1953]. 242 p. Mus.,
      port.
         Contents: "Argument d'après le drame de Georg Büchner," p. 9-
         30; "Introduction," p. 31-40; "Structure," p. 41-211; "Forme et
         invention," p. 215-242.
         Musical and dramatic analysis of the work, scene by scene.

555   Blaukopf, Kurt. "New light on Wozzeck," Saturday review 36:62, 76
      (Sept 26, 1953). Port.
         A description of "some recently discovered correspondence
         written by Alban Berg during his army career in World War I
         [which] gives strong evidence of Berg's personal identification
         with . . . Wozzeck."

556   Reich, Willi. "Alban Berg: 'Wozzeck'" in Oper im XX. Jahrhundert.
      Bonn, Boosey & Hawkes [c1954], p. 27-34. (Musik der Zeit: eine
      Schriftenreihe zur zeitgenössischen Musik, 6.)
         "Formgesinnung; Textgestaltung; Musikalischer Aufbau; Analy-
         tische Bemerkungen zu den einzelnen Szenen."

557   Kerman, Joseph. "Terror and self-pity: Alban Berg's Wozzeck;
      an analysis of a modern operatic masterpiece," Perspectives USA,
      no. 10:43-57 (Winter 1955).
         The style and mood of Wozzeck; a discussion of the opera as
         drama, not a musical analysis.

558   Kerman, Joseph. "Wozzeck and the Rake's progress" in his Opera
      as drama. New York, Knopf, c1956, p. 219-249. Mus.

Drawn from his earlier article (see no. 557). Comparison of Wozzeck with Stravinsky's opera. Reprinted by Vintage Books, 1959.

559   Newman, Ernest. "Wozzeck" in his From the world of music; essays from the Sunday Times. London, John Calder [1956], p. 148-159.
   Five brief essays, on the music, the drama, the first performance in England, and Berg's use of Sprechgesang.

560   Redlich, Hans. Ferdinand. "Wozzeck; Dramaturgie und musikalische Form," Musica 10:120-125 (Feb 1956).
   The layout of Büchner's text compared to Berg's; a table of the musical forms used in each scene.

See no. 509 (Berg, Alban. "A propos des formes employées dans Wozzeck" in his Ecrits, 1957, p. 109-117).

561   *Mahler, Fritz. Zu Alban Bergs Oper Wozzeck; szenische und musikalische Ubersicht. Wien, Universal Edition, c1957. 9 p. (See no. 549.)

562   Opera news v. 23, no. 19 (Mar 9, 1959), 33 p. Illus., mus.
   The entire issue is devoted to the Metropolitan Opera's first production of Wozzeck. Includes articles on the drama, the music, the singers, staging problems, Berg, and Büchner.

—act 3, scene 4

563   Jouve, Pierre Jean. "Wozzeck d'Alban Berg (Acte III, Scène IV)" in L'Oeuvre du XXe siècle. Paris, Richard-Masse, 1952, p. 87-98. Mus. (La revue musicale, no. 212.)
   An extract from his book (see no. 554).

ANTON WEBERN (1883-1945)

GENERAL

(Including Collections, Festschriften, etc.)

564   Anton Webern zum 50. Geburtstag.   23, eine Wiener musikzeitschrift no. 14 (Feb 1934), 25 p. Ports.
   Contents: "Zur Einleitung," p. 3; Webern, Anton, "Der Schönberg-schüler," p. 4-5; Reich, Willi, "Weberns Musik," p. 5-8; "Meister und Jünger," p. 8-9; Krenek, Ernst, "Freiheit und Verantwortung," p. 10-11; Humplik, Josef, "Dem Freunde," p. 12-13; Zenk, Ludwig, "Mein Lehrer," p. 13; Reich, Willi, "Weberns Vorträge," p. 17-22; "Die Presse," p. 22-23; Reich, Willi, "Lieber Freund Doktor Ploderer!" p. 24; "An die Leser," p.[25].

See no. 81 (Hijman, Julius. Nieuwe oostenrijkse musiek, 1938).

565   Leibowitz, René. "La musique: Anton Webern," L'arche, no. 11:130-134 (Nov 1945).
       Obituary; brief summary of life and works.

See no. 82 (Salazar, Adolfo. Music in our time, 1946).

566   Stein, Erwin. "Anton Webern," MT 87:14-15 (Jan 1946). Mus.
       An obituary. Brief discussion of Webern's works and style. Reprinted in Stein's Orpheus in new guises (see no. 303, p. 99-102).

See no. 297 (Bauer, Marion. Twentieth century music, 1947).

567   Dallapiccola, Luigi. "In memoria di Anton Webern," Emporium 105:18-20 (Jan 1947). Port.
       Obituary; biographical and critical article.

See no. 84 (Leibowitz, René. "Anton Webern: the awareness of the future in contemporary music" in his Schoenberg and his school, 1949, p. 187-255).

See no. 299 (Wörner, Karl H. Musik der Gegenwart, 1949).

568   Baruch, Gerth-Wolfgang. "Anton von Webern," Melos 20:337-342 (Dec 1953). Port.
       Biographical sketch; discussion of Webern's contributions. Includes a list of Webern's works, p. 342.

See no. 94 (Rognoni, Luigi. Espressionismo e dodecafonia, 1954).

569   Searle, Humphrey. "Webern, Anton (von)" in Grove's Dictionary of music and musicians. 5th ed., London, Macmillan, 1954, v. 9:225-228.
       Includes a bibliography and list of Webern's works.

570   Anton Webern. Tr. from the German by Leo Black, Eric Smith, and others. Bryn Mawr, Pa., Theodore Presser [c1955, 1958].
       vii + 100 p. Diagrs., illus., mus. (Die Reihe, a periodical devoted to developments in contemporary music, ed. by Herbert Eimert and Karlheinz Stockhausen, no. 2.)
            Contents: Stravinsky, Igor, "Foreword," p. vii; Wildgans, Friedrich, "Biographical table: index of works," p. 1-6; Jone, Hildegard, "A cantata," p. 7-8; Schoenberg, Arnold, "Foreword to Webern's Six Bagatelles, op. 6," p. 8; Webern, Anton, "Homage to Arnold Schoenberg," p. 9-10; "Anton Webern as a conductor," p. 11; Krenek, Ernst, "The same stone . . ." p. 12; "From the the correspondence [of Webern]," p. 13-21; Webern, Anton, "Choralis Constantinus," p. 23-25; Eimert, Herbert, "A change of focus," p. 29-36; Stockhausen, Karlheinz, "For the 15th of September, 1955," p. 37-39; Boulez, Pierre, "The threshold," p. 40-41; Metzger, Heinz-Klaus, "Webern and Schönberg," p. 42-45; Spinner, Leopold, "Analysis of a period: Concerto for 9 instruments, op. 24, second movement," p. 46-50; Pousseur, Henri, "Webern's organic chromaticism," p. 51-60; Wolff, Christian, "Movement," p. 61-63; Stockhausen, Karlheinz, "Structure and experimental time," p. 64-74; Metzger, Heinz-Klaus, "Analysis of the Sacred song, op. 15, no. 4," p. 75-80; Klammer, Armin,

"Webern's Piano variations, op. 27, 3rd movement," p. 81-92; Eimert, Herbert, "Interval proportions: String quartet, 1st movement," p. 93-99; "The published works of Anton Webern," p. 100. A lengthy review of this symposium, by Peter Stadlen, is found in Score, no. 25:65-68 (Jun 1959).

See no. 100 (Collaer, Paul. La musique moderne, 1905-1955. 1955).

See no. 105 (Hamilton, Iain. "Alban Berg and Anton Webern" in Hartog, Howard, ed. European music in the twentieth century, 1957, p. 94-117).

571   Stuckenschmidt, Hans Heinz. "Anton Webern," Ricordiana [nuova serie] 3:274-277 (Jun 1957).
      Brief résumé of his life and works.

See no. 112 (Prieberg, Fred K. Lexikon der neuen Musik, 1958, p. 446-449).

See no. 115 (Stuckenschmidt, Hans Heinz. "Anton von Webern" in his Schöpfer der neuen Musik, 1958, p. 192-203).

See no. 116 (Vlad, Roman. "I traguardi del radicalismo di Webern" in his Storia della dodecafonia, 1958, p. 125-130).

572   Adorno, Theodor Wiesengrund. "Anton von Webern" in his Klangfiguren. Berlin, Suhrkamp, c1959, p. 157-181. (His Musikalische Schriften, I.)
      "Ursprünglich ein Vortrag für den Norddeutschen Rundfunk, veröffentlicht in 'Merkur,' 13. Jahrg., Heft 3, März 1959, S. 201 ff."

See no. 118a (Zillig, Winfried. "Anton Webern, Aussenseiter und Vorbild" in his Variationen über neue Musik, 1959, p. 181-190).

PHILOSOPHY AND CRITICISM

573   Adorno, Theodor Wiesengrund. "Anton Webern: zur Aufführung der fünf Orchesterstücke in Zürich," Musikblätter des Anbruch 8:280-282 (May 1926).
      Very general essay on Webern's music; not an analysis.

574   List, Kurt. "Anton von Webern," Modern music 21:27-30 (Nov/Dec 1943).
      An essay in honor of Webern's 60th birthday; the character of his music.

575   Leibowitz, René. "Innovation and tradition in contemporary music: II. The tragic art of Anton Webern," Horizon [London] 15:282-293 (May 1947).
      Similar to his article on Schoenberg in this series (see no. 320), but somewhat more technical regarding row technique.

576   Craft, Robert. "Discoveries and convictions," Counterpoint 18:16-18
       (Feb 1953).
           Review of an all-Webern concert and discussion of the essential
       points of Webern's music.

See no. 29 (Goléa, Antoine. Esthétique de la musique contemporaine,
       1954, p. 63-66).

577   Maren, Roger. "The music of Anton Webern: prisms in twelve
       tones," Reporter 16:38-41 (May 30, 1957).
           A review of the recording of Webern's complete works; also
       some general comments about Webern's style and about the
       twelve-tone technique.

See no. 170 (Pousseur, Henri. "Webern und die Theorie" in Steinecke,
       Wolfgang, ed. Darmstädter Beiträge zur neuen Musik, 1958, p. 38-
       43).

578   Wildgans, Friedrich. "Anton von Webern; zu seinem 75. Geburts-
       tag am 3. Dezember 1958," ÖMZ 13:456-460 (Nov 1958). Illus.
       (autograph of a Webern MS), port.
           Webern's posthumous influence and importance.

579   Hampton, Christopher. "Anton Webern and the consciousness of
       time," Mus rev 20:45-51 (Feb 1959).
           An interpretation of the importance of Webern.

                              BIOGRAPHY

580   Searle, Humphrey. "Conversations with Webern," MT 81:405-406
       (Oct 1940).
           Searle's experiences as a student of Webern. Includes a list of
       Webern's works through op. 29.

See no. 83 (Schlee, Alfred. "Vienna since the Anschluss," Spring 1946).

See no. 569 (Anton Webern. 1955, 1958 [Die Reihe, 2]).

580a Dorian, Frederick Deutsch. "Webern als Lehrer," Melos 27:101-106
       (Apr 1960). Port.
           Webern as a teacher.

                           CORRESPONDENCE

See no. 374 (Hill, Richard S. "Annual reports on acquisitions: music,"
       Nov 1952).

See no. 511 (Reich, Willi. "Aus unbekannten Briefen von Alban Berg an
       Anton Webern," Feb 1953).

See no. 569 ("From the correspondence" in Anton Webern, 1955, 1958,
       p. 13-21 [Die Reihe, 2]).

581   Gerhard, Roberto, ed. "Letters of Webern and Schoenberg" [to Roberto Gerhard], Score, no. 24:36-41 (Nov 1958).
       These letters date from 1931-1934.

582   Webern, Anton von. Briefe an Hildegard Jone und Josef Humplik. Hrsg. von Josef Polnauer. Wien, Universal Edition, 1959, 106 p. Port., mus.
       Extensive explanatory notes included.

COMPOSITIONAL TECHNIQUES

583   Stein, Erwin. "Anton Webern," Anbruch 13:107-109 (Jun/Jul 1931). Mus.
       A brief and general discussion of his compositional techniques.

See no. 569 (Anton Webern. 1955, 1958 [Die Reihe, 2]).

See no. 154 (Erickson, Robert. The structure of music, 1955).

584   Vlad, Roman. "Anton von Webern e la composizione atematica," Rass mus 25:98-102 (Apr/Jun 1955). Mus.
       The replacement of thematic content in Webern's works by structural design. Deals especially with the Concerto for 9 instruments, op. 24; the Variations for piano, op. 27; and the Variations for orchestra, op. 30.
       An extract from chapter 7 of Vlad's Storia della dodecafonia (see no. 116).

See no. 43 (Rochberg, George. "Tradition and twelve-tone music," Dec 1955).

See no. 160 (Perle, George. Serial composition and atonality, 1956).

585   Stephan, Rudolph. "Anton von Webern," Dt Univ Zt 13/14:26-29 (Jul 19, 1956). Mus.
       General discussion of Webern's works and compositional technique, including use of the row.

586   Pousseur, Henri. "Da Schoenberg a Webern: una mutazione," Incontri musicali 1:3-39 (Dec 1956), tr. by Vittorio Armanni. Mus.
       A continuation of his study of Webern begun in Die Reihe, 2 (see no. 569, p. 51-60), and a comparison of Webern's and Schoenberg's compositional techniques. Examples from Schoenberg's op. 19 and 30 and from Webern's op. 5, 16, 26, 27 and other works.

GENERAL DESCRIPTIONS OF WORKS

587   Evans, Edwin. "Webern, Anton von" in Cobbett, Walter W. Cobbett's cyclopedic survey of chamber music. London, Oxford University Press, 1929/30, p. 571-574. Mus.

Discusses, very briefly, the Five movements for string quartet, the Four pieces for violin and piano, the Six bagatelles for string quartet, and the Three little pieces for cello and piano.

588   Reich, Willi. "Anton von Webern," Die Musik 22:812-816 (Aug 1930). Description of works through 1929.

See no. 516 (Adorno, Theodor Wiesengrund. "Berg and Webern—Schoenberg's heirs," Jan 1931).

See no. 484 (Leibowitz, René. "Les dernières oeuvres de Schoenberg, de Webern, et de Berg" in his Introduction à la musique de douze sons, 1949, p. 232-244).

See no. 403 (Demuth, Norman. Musical trends in the twentieth century, 1952, p. 233-238).

589   "Oeuvres d'Anton Webern (1883-1945)," Music information record 11:17-18 (Winter 1953/54). Lists of works with dates of publication.

See no. 95 (Wörner, Karl H. Neue Musik in der Entscheidung, 1954, p. 94-98).

590   Stephan, Rudolf. "Über einige geistliche Kompositionen Anton von Weberns," Musik und Kirche 24:152-160 (Jul/Aug 1954). Mus. Discussion and analysis of op. 15, 16, 17, 18, 23, 26, 29, 31.

See no. 155 (Ogdon, Wilbur Lee. Series and structure, 1955).

591   Craft, Robert. "Anton Webern," Score, no. 13:9-22 (Sept 1955). Biographical sketch; brief discussion of each group of works, and a list of Webern's compositions, with timings.

See no. 586 (Pousseur, Henri. "Da Schoenberg a Webern," Dec 1956).

592   Mason, Colin. "Webern's later chamber music," M & L 38:232-237 (Jul 1957). A discussion of the chamber works from op. 15 on.

INDIVIDUAL WORKS

Bagatelles for string quartet, op. 9

See no. 569 (Schoenberg, Arnold. "Foreword to Webern's Six bagatelles, op. 6" in Anton Webern, 1955, 1958, p. 8 [Die Reihe, 2]).

Cantatas
—no. 2, op. 31

593   Mason, Colin. "New music," Chesterian 26:25-27 (Oct 1951). Review of the score; some analytical comments, especially concerning the row structure.

594   Castiglioni, Niccolò. "Sul rapporto tra parola e musica nella
      seconda Cantata di Webern," Incontri musicali, no. 3:112-127 (Aug
      1959).
         Includes a translation of the text of the cantata into Italian.

Concerto for 9 instruments, op. 24

595   Leibowitz, René. Qu'est-ce que la musique de douze sons? Le
      concerto pour neuf instruments, op. 24, d'Anton Webern. Liège,
      Editions Dynamo, 1948. 63 p. + 8 p. "exemples musicaux."
         Contents: "Le sens des problèmes soulevés par Schoenberg,"
         p. 8-15; "L'évolution d'Anton Webern," p. 16-18; "Le concerto
         pour neuf instruments, op. 24, d'Anton Webern," p. 19-53; "Con-
         clusion: les possibilités de reconnaissance d'une oeuvre," p. 55-
         61.
         Includes a theme-by-theme analysis of the concerto.

See no. 584 (Vlad, Roman. "Anton von Webern e la composizione atema-
      tica," Apr/Jun 1955).

—First movement

596   Stockhausen, Karlheinz. "Weberns Konzert für 9 Instrumente, op.
      24; Analyse der ersten Satzes," Melos 20:343-348 (Dec 1953). Mus.
      Interesting not only as a detailed analysis of the Webern, but
      also as an example of Stockhausen's analytical technique.

—Second movement

See no. 569 (Spinner, Leopold. "Analysis of a period: Concerto for 9
      instruments, op. 24, second movement" in Anton Webern, 1955,
      1958, p. 46-50 [Die Reihe, 2]).

Five movements for string quartet, op. 5
         See his Movements for string quartet, op. 5

Five orchestral pieces, op. 10
         See his Orchestral pieces, op. 10

Five sacred songs, op. 15
         See his Songs—op. 15

Geistliche Lieder, op. 15
         See his Songs—op. 15

Klavier Variationen, op. 27
         See his Variations for piano, op. 27

Movements for string quartet, op. 5

597   Asuar, José Vicente. "Una incursion por el Op. 5 di Anton Webern,"
      Revista musicale chilena 12:19-41 (Mar/Apr 1958). Mus.
      A detailed analysis.

Orchestral pieces, op. 10

See no. 573 (Adorno, Theodor Wiesengrund. "Anton Webern: zur Aufführ-
      ung der fünf Orchesterstücke in Zürich," May 1926).

Orchestral variations, op. 30
      See his Variations for orchestra, op. 30

Passacaglia for orchestra, op. 1

See no. 456 (Cowell, Henry. "Current chronicle: New York," Jan 1949).

Piano quintet (1907)
      See his Quintet, piano and strings

Piano variations, op. 27
      See his Variations for piano, op. 27

Quartet, strings, op. 28

598   Wellesz, Egon. "Reviews of music: Webern, Anton, String Quartet,
      op. 28," Mus rev 1:177-178 (May 1940).
          An interesting contemporary review; brief discussion of "atonality"
      and the twelve-tone technique; mention of the main musical ideas
      of the quartet.

See no. 206 (Johnson, Martha. A study of linear design, 1954).

599   Elston, Arnold. "Some rhythmic practices in contemporary music,"
      MQ 42:318-329 (Jul 1956). Mus.
          Webern, p. 325-329.

—First movement

See no. 569 (Eimert, Herbert. "Interval proportions: string quartet, first
      movement" in Anton Webern, 1955, 1958, p. 93-99 [Die Reihe, 2]).

—Second movement

See no. 569 (Stockhausen, Karlheinz. "Structure and experimental time"
      in Anton Webern, 1955, 1958, p. 64-74 [Die Reihe, 2]).

Quintet, piano and strings (1907)

600   Newlin, Dika. "Music reviews; Anton von Webern: Quintet for
      string quartet and piano," Notes 10:674-675 (Sept 1953).
      General comments about the structure and "style."

Sacred songs, op. 15
      See his Songs—op. 15

Sätze für Streichquartet, op. 5
      See his Movements for string quartet, op. 5

Songs

See no. 590 (Stephan, Rudolf. "Über einige geistliche Kompositionen
      Anton von Weberns," Jul/Aug 1954).

See no. 476 (Zeiger, Jean Wilson. Early expressionistic songs, 1959).

601   Mayer, Harry. "De liedkunst van Anton Webern," Mens en melodie
      14:114-117 (Apr 1959). Mus., port.
      A brief discussion of his songs.

—op. 4 (Five songs)
      —op. 4:2

See no. 476 (Zeiger, Jean Wilson. Early expressionistic songs, 1959).

—op. 15 (Five sacred songs)
      —op. 15:4

See no. 569 (Metzger, Heinz-Klaus. "Analysis of the sacred song, op. 15,
      no. 4" in Anton Webern, 1955, 1958, p. 75-80 [Die Reihe, 2]).

See no. 476 (Zeiger, Jean Wilson. Early expressionistic songs, 1959).

—op. 23 (Three songs)

See no. 526 (Bach, David Joseph. "New music by Berg, Webern, Krenek,"
      Nov/Dec 1934).

String quartet, op. 28
      See his Quartet, strings, op. 28

String quartet, Six bagatelles for
      See his Bagatelles for string quartet, op. 9

Stücke für Orchester, op. 10
      See his Orchestral pieces, op. 10

Three songs with piano accompaniment, op. 23
    See his Songs—op. 23

Variations for orchestra, op. 30

See no. 584 (Vlad, Roman. "Anton von Webern e la composizione atemati-
    ca," Apr/Jun 1955).

See no. 170 (Nono, Luigi. "Die Entwicklung der Reihentechnik" in Stein-
    ecke, Wolfgang, ed. Darmstädter Beiträge zur neuen Musik, 1958,
    p. 25-37).

Variations for piano, op. 27

See no. 155 (Ogdon, Wilbur Lee. Series and structure, 1955).

See no. 584 (Vlad, Roman. "Anton von Webern e la composizione atemati-
    ca," Apr/Jun 1955).

See no. 57 (Stadlen, Peter. "Serialism reconsidered," Feb 1958).

See no. 59 (Gerhard, Roberto. "Apropos Mr. Stadlen," Jul 1958).

See no. 66 (Stadlen, Peter. "No real casualties?" Nov 1958).

—third movement

See no. 569 (Klammer, Armin. "Webern's Piano variations, op. 27, 3rd
    movement" in Anton Webern, 1955, 1958, p. 81-92 [Die Reihe, 2]).

IV
OTHER COMPOSERS

MILTON BABBITT

602   Bruno, Anthony. "Two American twelve-tone composers: Milton Babbitt and Ben Weber represent opposing views," Musical America 71:22, 170 (Feb 1951).
Row technique as used by the two composers.

See no. 99a (Chase, Gilbert. "Twelve tone composers" in his America's music, 1955).

See no. 204a (Rochberg, George. "The harmonic tendency of the hexachord," Nov 1959).

All set

603   Gottlieb, Louis. "Brandeis festival album," Jazz: a quarterly of American music, no. 2:151-160 (Spring 1959). Mus.
Brief serial analysis of All set, p. 152-156.

Quartet, woodwinds

604   Rochberg, George. "Music reviews; Milton Babbitt: Woodwind quartet in one movement," Notes 13:695-696 (Sept 1956).
Capsule description of Babbitt's structural procedures.

LUCIANO BERIO

See no. 106 (Pestalozza, Luigi. "I compositori milanesi del dopoguerra," Mar 1957).

605   "Luciano Berio," Schw MZ 97:233 (Jun 1957).
Very brief list of works, with dates.

See no. 112 (Prieberg, Fred K. Lexikon der neuen Musik, 1958, p. 42).

See no. 116 (Vlad, Roman. Storia della dodecafonia, 1958, p. 262-263, 268).

See no. 118a (Zillig, Winfried. "Die Jungen: Stockhausen, Boulez, Nono, Berio" in his Variationen über neuen Musik, 1959, p. 190-199).

See no. 637 (Metzger, Heinz-Klaus. "John Cage o della liberazione,"
Aug 1959).

Alleluia

606   Berio, Luciano. "Aspetti di artigianato formale," Incontri musicali
1:55-69 (Dec 1956). Mus.
A detailed explanation of the organizing principles of this work.

607   Thomas, Ernst. "Ein 'Allelujah' aus dem Jahre 1956," NZfM 118:
433-434 (Jul/Aug 1957).
A very brief review, giving some background on Berio.

Nones

See no. 168 (Santi, Piero. "Luciano Berio" in Junge Komponisten, 1958,
p. 98-102 [Die Reihe, 4]).

608   Smith Brindle, Reginald. "Current chronicle: Italy," MQ 44:95-101
(Jan 1958). Mus.
An explanation of the principle of "total control," with examples
drawn from the beginning of the work.

Quartet, string

See no. 168 (Santi, Piero. "Luciano Berio" in Junge Komponisten, 1958,
p. 98-102 [Die Reihe, 4]).

Sequenza per flauto solo

See no. 71 (Eco, Umberto. "L'opera in movimento e la coscienza
dell'epoca," Aug 1959).

Thema: Omaggio a Joyce

609   Berio, Luciano. "Poesie e musica—un'esperienza," Incontri musicali,
no. 3:98-111 (Aug 1959). Diagrs.
Experiments in new means of combining text and music; Berio's
setting of the begginning of the 11th chapter of Joyce's Ulysses
(see no. 174).

PIERRE BOULEZ

GENERAL

610   Goldbeck, Frederick. "Current chronicle: France," MQ 36:291-295
(Apr 1950). Mus.
One of the first articles on "totally controlled" serial music.

611   Scriabine, Marina. "Pierre Boulez et la musique concrète" in Les carnets critiques. Paris, Richard-Masse [1952], p. 14-15. (La revue musicale, no. 215.)
      Boulez as organizer of electronic experiments in the Paris Studio.

612   Goldbeck, Fred E. "Boulez, Pierre" in Grove's Dictionary of music and musicians. 5th ed. London, Macmillan, 1954, v. 1: 844.
      Includes a very brief list of selected works.

See no. 29 (Goléa, Antoine. Esthétique de la musique contemporaine, 1954, p. 176-189, 193).

See no. 30 (La musique et ses problèmes contemporains, 1954, p. 3-24).

See no. 98 (Myers, Rollo H. "Music in France in the post-war decade," 1954/55).

613   Myers, Rollo H. "Some personalities and trends in contemporary French music," Chesterian 30:14-18 (Jul 1955).
      Boulez, p. 16-17.

614   Hodeir, Andre. "The young French music," Saturday review 40:41-42, 53 (May 25, 1957), tr. by David Noakes. Port.
      Brief summary of Boulez's musical philosophy, p. 42, 53.

615   Goléa, Antoine. Rencontres avec Pierre Boulez, avec trois hors-texte. Paris, R. Julliard [1958]. 259 p. Port., facsims., mus.
      A lengthy discussion of Boulez's life, works, compositional techniques, and aesthetics. Difficult to use: no table of contents, chapter headings, or index.

See no. 112 (Prieberg, Fred K. Lexicon der neuen Musik, 1958, p. 53-55).

See no. 116 (Vlad, Roman. Storia della dodecafonia, 1958, p. 257-261).

616   Lesure, François. "Profili di musicisti contemporanei," Musica d'oggi 1:19-21 (Jan 1958).
      Principally a discussion of his musical philosophy; includes a list of works.

See no. 118a (Zillig, Winfried. "Die Jungen: Stockhausen, Boulez, Nono, Berio" in his Variationen über neuen Musik, 1959, p. 190-199).

See no. 637 (Metzger, Heinz-Klaus. "John Cage o della liberazione," Aug 1959).

COMPOSITIONAL TECHNIQUES

See no. 208 (Boulez, Pierre. "Propositions" in Le rythme musical, 1948, p. 65-72 [Polyphonie, 2^e cahier]).

617   Cowell, Henry. "Current chronicle: New York," MQ 38:132-134 (Jan 1952). Illus., mus.
      Boulez's serial technique and its relation to the experiments of John Cage.

See no. 150 (Krenek, Ernst. "Is the twelve-tone technique on the decline?"
Oct 1953).
Discusses Boulez's Piano sonata no. 2 and his Polyphonie X.

618   Barraqué, Jean. "Rythme et développement" in Inventaire des techniques rédactionnelles. Paris, Richard-Masse [1954], p. 47-73.
(Polyphonie, 9e/10e cahier.)
Boulez, p. 63-73. Examples from his Piano sonata no. 2, String
quartet, and Polyphonie pour 18 instruments.

INDIVIDUAL WORKS

Le marteau sans maître

619   Saathen, Friedrich. "'Le Marteau sans maître' von Pierre Boulez,"
Schw MZ 97:289-290 (Jul 1957).
Not an analysis. Discusses Boulez's musical philosophy. Includes
a German translation of the text of 'Le marteau.'

See no. 170 (Stockhausen, Karlheinz. "Sprache und Musik" in Steinecke,
Wolfgang, ed. Darmstädter Beiträge zur neuen Musik, 1958, p. 57-
81).

620   Mason, Colin. "Reviews of music," M & L 39:198-199 (Apr 1958).
Mus.
Brief review, indicating the rhythmic complexity of the work.

621   Craft, Robert. "Boulez and Stockhausen," Score, no. 24:54-62 (Nov
1958).
"Notes written in the course of preparing a record . . . for
American Columbia." Principally discusses influences and structure.

622   Skulsky, Abraham. "After Webern, who?" American record guide
23:316-319 (Jan 1959). Illus.
Description for the layman of Boulez's and Stockhausen's compositional techniques; review of the recording.

L'Orestie

623   Rostand, Claude, "La musique de scène de Pierre Boulez pour
'L'Orestie' d'Eschyle," Schw MZ 96:11-13 (Jan 1956). Mus.
Discusses declamation of the text and theatrical effect.

Poésie pour pouvoir

624   Heck, Ludwig. "Klänge in Schmelztiegel," Melos 25:320-329 (Oct
1958). Diagrs., illus.
Technological problems encountered in setting up Boulez's Poésie
pour pouvoir, a piece combining three orchestras and electroni-
cally produced sounds.

625   Wörner, Karl H. "Current chronicle: Germany," MQ 45:239-241 (Apr 1959).
A brief description of the work.

Polyphonie X for 18 solo instruments

626   Morton, Lawrence. "Los Angeles letter," Counterpoint 17:33-34 (Nov 1952).
A review and general summary.

Sonatas, piano
—no. 2

627   Demuth, Norman. French piano music; a survey with notes on its performance. London, Museum Press [c1959]. 179 p. Mus.
Boulez, p. 152-156; a brief description of the Sonata.

—no. 3

628   Ligeti, György. "Zur III. Klaviersonate von Boulez" in Berichte/Analysen. Wien, Universal Edition [c1959], p. 38-40. (Die Reihe, 5.)
Very brief; no musical examples.

Sonatina, flute and piano

629   Pestalozzi, Luigi. "Vita musicale: musiche nuovissime," Rass mus 26:298-299 (Oct 1956).
Review of the first concert of the Incontri Musicali in Milan.

Structures, for two pianos, four hands

630   Vlad, Roman. "Recensioni: Pierre Boulez, Structures per 2 pianoforti a 4 mani," Rass mus 26:153-155 (Apr 1956).
General review; not an analysis.

See no. 170 (Nono, Luigi. "Die Entwicklung der Reihentechnik" in Steinecke, Wolfgang, ed. Darmstädter Beiträge zur neuen Musik, 1958, p. 25-37).

—no. 1a

See no. 168 (Ligeti, György. "Pierre Boulez" in Junge Komponisten, 1958, p. 38-63 [Die Reihe, 4]).

631   Wilkinson, Mark. "Pierre Boulez' 'Structure 1a': Bemerkungen zur Zwölfton-technik/Some thoughts on twelve-tone method," Gravesaner Blätter, Heft 10:12-29 (1958). Tables.
In German (p. 12-18) and English (p. 23-29). An analysis of the serial technique in the Structure 1a.

JOHN CAGE

632   Cowell, Henry. "Current chronicle: New York," MQ 38:123-127 (Jan 1952).
Cage's rhythmic structural principles. Discusses his Imaginary landscape and Music of changes. Influences on Morton Feldman and Pierre Boulez.

633   Glanville-Hicks, Peggy. "Cage, John" in Grove's Dictionary of music and musicians. 5th ed. London, Macmillan, 1954, v. 2:16-17.
Includes a list of his works.

See no. 29 (Goléa, Antoine. Esthétique de la musique contemporaine, 1954, p. 183-184).

634   Curjel, Hans. "Cage oder das wohlpräparierte Klavier," Melos 22:97-100 (Apr 1955). Illus., port.
One of the few articles attempting to evaluate Cage's experiments seriously.

635   Cage, John. "Experimental music," Score, no. 12:65-68 (Jun 1955).
Rather whimsical article in dialogue form, discussing Cage's style.

See no. 253 (Boulez, Pierre. "Tendances de la musique récente" in Vers une musique expérimentale, 1957, p. 28-35).

See no. 112 (Prieberg, Fred K. Lexikon der neuen Musik, 1958, p. 67-68).

636   Maren, Roger. "The musical numbers game," Reporter 18:37-39 (Mar 6, 1958).
The compositional philosophies of Cage and of Stockhausen.

See no. 63 (Porena, Boris. "L'avanguardia musicale di Darmstadt," Sept 1958).

637   Metzger, Heinz-Klaus. "John Cage o della liberazione," Incontri musicali, no. 3:16-31 (Aug 1959), tr. by Sylvano Bussotti.
Cage's aesthetic philosophy; freedom of choice for the performer in Cage's works; similar techniques in Stockhausen, Boulez, Berio, Pousseur.

Music for piano 21-52

See no. 166 (Cage, John. "To describe the process of composition used in 'Music for piano 21-52'" in Musical craftsmanship, 1957, 1959, p. 41-43 [Die Reihe, 3]).

Sonata, piano, no. 4

See no. 87 (Thomson, Virgil. "Atonality today," Nov 1951).

LUIGI DALLAPICCOLA

GENERAL

638   Searle, Humphrey. "Luigi Dallapiccola," Listener 40:780 (Nov 18, 1948).
     Brief discussion of some of his works; his background and influences.

639   Skulsky, Abraham. "Dallapiccola felt impelled to introduce a new romantic era," Musical America 69:6, 40-41 (May 1949). Port.
     Brief discussion of his life and works.

640   Dallapiccola, Luigi. "Sulla strada della dodecafonia," Aut aut 1:30-45 (Jan 1951).

        _____. "On the twelve-note road," Mus sur 4:318-332 (Oct 1951).
     Dallapiccola's account of his adoption of the twelve-tone technique; the character of dodecaphony (especially compared with literary techniques, e.g., Joyce and Proust).

641   Mila, Massimo. "Dallapiccola, Luigi" in Die Musik in Geschichte und Gegenwart. Kassel, Bärenreiter, 1952. v. 2, col. 1874-1875, tr. by Anna Amalie Abert. Mus.
     Includes a bibliography and a list of works.

642   Amico, Fedele d'. "Luigi Dallapiccola," Melos 20:69-74 (Mar 1953). Illus., port.
     Biographical sketch; general discussion of his works and style, through 1952.

643   Gatti, Guido M. "Dallapiccola, Luigi" in Grove's Dictionary of music and musicians. 5th ed. London, Macmillan, 1954, v. 2:582-583.
     Includes a list of his works; no bibliography.

See no. 29 (Goléa, Antoine. Esthétique de la musique contemporaine, 1954, p. 143-147).

See no. 151 ("Contemporary composers on their experiences of composition with twelve notes: Luigi Dallapiccola" in Rufer, Josef. Composition with twelve notes, 1954, p. 178-181).

See no. 100 (Collaer, Paul. La musique moderne, 1905-1955. 1955, p. 272-274).

See no. 105 (Smith Brindle, Reginald. "Italian contemporary music" in Hartog, Howard, ed. European music in the twentieth century, 1957, p. 176-181).

See no. 112 (Prieberg, Fred K. Lexikon der neuen Musik, 1958, p. 87-90).

See no. 115 (Stuckenschmidt, Hans Heinz. Schöpfer der neuen Musik, 1958, p. 228-240).

See no. 118a (Zillig, Winfried. "Die Erneuerung der italienischen Musik von Malipiero bis Dallapiccola" in his Variationen über neue Musik, 1959, p. 165-173).

GENERAL DESCRIPTIONS OF WORKS

644 Paoli, Domenico de. "Chroniques et notes; Italie: Luigi Dallapiccola,"
Rev mus 16:65-67 (Jun 1935).
Brief general article on Dallapiccola's early works.

645 "Voci aggiunte a un dizionario dei musicisti italiani contemporanei:
Luigi Dallapiccola," Rass mus 9/10:284-285 (Sept/Oct 1936) and
20:40-41 (Jan 1950).
A list of his works.

646 Ballo, Ferdinando. "Le musiche chorali di Dallapiccola," Rass mus
10:136-141 (Apr 1937).
The early choral works; a general essay, not an analysis.

647 "Un musicien d'aujourd'hui: Luigi Dallapiccola" in Le théâtre musical. Paris, Richard-Masse [1947/48]. (Polyphonie, 1er cahier.)
Mus., port.
Contents: "Chronologie et portrait," p. 135-138 (gives dates of
performances); Dallapiccola, Luigi, "Notes sur mon opéra,"
p. 139-142 (on Il prigioniero); "Bibliographie," p. 143-146 (list
of compositions with dates of first performance, timings, and
publishers); "Supplement musical hors-texte: 'La canzona dei
Pezzenti,' extraite de 'Il prigioniero,' opéra de L. Dallapiccola."

648 Vlad, Roman. "Luigi Dallapiccola," Horizon [London] 20:379-391
(Dec 1949/Jan 1950), tr. by Toni del Renzio.
A discussion of his works through the Due pezzi.

649 Gavazzeni, Gianandrea. Musicisti d'Europa: studi sui contemporanei.
[Milano] Suvini Zerboni [1954]. 275 p.
A collection of critical essays on various composers. Studi su
Dallapiccola, p. 191-224: "Cori e laudi" (1937), p. 191-201; "Dai
Canti di prigionia a Rencesvals" (1946), p. 202-218; "Il piccolo
concerto per Muriel Couvreux" (1943), p. 219-224.

650 Valentin, Erich. "Klassiker aus antikem Geist: Luigi Dallapiccola
fünfzig Jahre," ZfM 115:94-95 (Feb 1954).
A brief survey of his works.

See no. 35 (Vlad, Roman. Modernità e tradizione nella musica contemporanea, 1955, p. 197-211).

651 Vlad, Roman. "Dallapiccola, 1948-55," Score, no. 15:39-62 (Mar
1956). Mus.
A continuation of the survey of Dallapiccola's works (begun in
his article in Horizon; see no. 648) through the cantata An
Mathilde (1955). Includes a complete score of Dallapiccola's
Improvisation after Tartini, for violin and piano, p. 56-62.

652 Vlad, Roman. Luigi Dallapiccola. Tr. by Cynthia Jolly. Milano,
Suvini Zerboni, 1957. 62 p. Mus.
Biographical sketch, p. 60; list of works, p. 61-62. A translation
of the Dallapiccola chapter from his Storia della dodecafonia
(see no. 116), p. 275-314.

653   Nathan, Hans. "The twelve-tone compositions of Luigi Dallapiccola,"
      MQ 44:289-310 (Jul 1958). Mus.
          A list of his "completely dodecaphonic" compositions, p. 309-310.
          A general discussion, with musical illustrations, of Dallapiccola's
          style and the main influences that have shaped it.

654   Basart, Ann P.   The twelve-tone compositions of Luigi Dallapiccola.
      (Thesis, M. A., University of California, 1960.) iii + 117 l. Mus.
          Contents: "Il prigioniero," p. 7-29; "Quaderno musicale di Anna-
          libera," p. 30-55; "Canti di liberazione," p. 56-78; "Cinque canti
          per baritono," p. 79-99; "Conclusions," p. 110-113. Primarily an
          analysis.

                        INDIVIDUAL WORKS

                          An Mathilde

655   Mila, Massimo. "L'incontro Heine-Dallapiccola," Rass mus 27:301-
      308 (Dec 1957). Mus.
          Somewhat extensive analysis, with emphasis on the textual mean-
          ing as reflected in the music.

                       Canti di liberazione

See no. 161 (Smith Brindle, Reginald. "The lunatic fringe, III: computa-
      tional composition," Jul 1956).

656   Vlad, Roman. "Vita musicale: Roma," Rass mus 27:54-55 (Mar 1957).
          Gives some background of the text; a general review.

657   Smith Brindle, Reginald. "Current chronicle: Italy," MQ 43:240-245
      (Apr 1957). Mus.
          Emphasis on the rhythmic structure.

658   Drew, David. "The arts and entertainment: Dallapiccola," New
      statesman 57:363-365 (Mar 14, 1959).
          Discusses the Canti di liberazione in relation to the other
          works of his trilogy on prisoners and freedom.

See no. 654 (Basart, Ann P. "Canti di liberazione" in her The twelve-
      tone compositions of Luigi Dallapiccola, 1960, p. 56-78).

                        Canti di prigionia

659   Amico, Fedele d'. "'Canti di prigionia,'" Società [Roma] 1:95-100
      (Jan/Jun 1945).
          Philosophical background of the work.

See no. 669 (Goldman, Richard Franco. "Current chronicle: New York,"
      Jul 1951).

660   Morton, Lawrence. "Los Angeles letter," Counterpoint 18:35-36 (Feb 1953).
      A brief review.

See no. 670 (Dallapiccola, Luigi. "The genesis of the Canti di prigionia and Il prigioniero," Jul 1953).

Cinque canti per baritono

661   Wildberger, Jacques. "Dallapiccolas 'Cinque Canti,'" Melos 26:7-10 (Jan 1959). Mus.
      Brief analysis, especially of serial and rhythmic structure.

See no. 654 (Basart, Ann P. "Cinque canti per baritono" in her The twelve-tone compositions of Luigi Dallapiccola, 1960, p. 79-99).

Greek lyrics
See his Liriche greche

Improvisation after Tartini, for violin and piano

See no. 651 (Vlad, Roman. "Dallapiccola, 1948-55," Mar 1956, p. 56-62).

Job, una sacra rappresentazione

662   Wörner, Karl H. "Dallapiccolas Job," Melos 21:208-210 (Jul/Aug 1954). Mus.
      An excellent article on the musical structure and on the implications of the drama. Gives, however, an incorrect quotation of the principal twelve-note row.

663   Skulsky, Abraham. "Opera, 1954," Juilliard review 2:34-43 (Winter, 1955). Mus.
      Job, p. 37-38. Brief summary of the musical and dramatic structure; one page from the full score is reproduced.

Liriche greche

664   Amico, Fedele d'. "Recensioni: Luigi Dallapiccola," Rass mus 17:165-170 (Apr 1947).
      A general review; no musical examples.

Marsia

665   Gatti, Guido M. "Current chronicle: Italy," MQ 35:136-139 (Jan 1949). Mus.
      Review of a performance at Venice; background of the work, brief sketch of the central dramatic and musical ideas.

666   Smith Brindle, Reginald. "Current chronicle: Italy," MQ 41:524-526 (Oct 1955).
      Gives a capsule idea of the character of this ballet.

Orchestral variations
See his Variations for orchestra

Il prigioniero

See no. 647 (Dallapiccola, Luigi. "Notes sur mon opéra" in Le théâtre musical, 1947/48, p. 139-142 [Polyphonie, 1]).

667   Keller, Hans. "XIII Maggio musicale fiorentino," Mus rev 11:211 (Aug 1950).
A psychological approach to the text.

668   Mila, Massimo. "'Il prigioniero' di Luigi Dallapiccola," Rass mus 20:303-311 (Oct 1950). Mus.
Background of the libretto; discussion of the music, including row technique.

669   Goldman, Richard F. "Current chronicle, New York," MQ 37:405-410 (Jul 1951). Mus.
A comparison of the opera with the Canti di prigionia; discussion of the text and the musical materials.

670   Dallapiccola, Luigi. "The genesis of the Canti di prigionia and Il prigioniero: an autobiographical fragment," MQ 39:355-372 (Jul 1953), tr. by Jonathan Schiller. Port.
The origins of the central ideas of these works from literature and from events in Dallapiccola's life.

671   Rufer, Josef. "Luigi Dallapiccola: Il prigioniero" in Oper im XX. Jahrhundert. Bonn, Boosey & Hawkes [c1954], p. 56-64. Illus., mus. (Musik der Zeit: eine Schriftenreihe zur zeitgenössischen Musik, 6.)
Brief background on the development of Italian music in the 20th century; sketch of the plot and of the central musical ideas of Il prigioniero.

672   Mason, Colin. "Dallapiccola and the twelve-note method," Listener 51:757 (Apr 29, 1954).
The use of dodecaphony in Il prigioniero.

See no. 35 (Vlad, Roman. "'Il prigioniero'" in his Modernità e tradizione nella musica contemporanea, 1955, p. 212-216).

See no. 654 (Basart, Ann P. "Il prigioniero" in her The twelve-tone compositions of Luigi Dallapiccola, 1960, p. 7-29).

Quaderno musicale di Annalibera
See also his Variations for orchestra

673   Keller, Hans. "The half-year's new music," Mus rev 15:214-215 (Aug 1954).
An outline sketch of the form and techniques used.

See no. 654 (Basart, Ann P. "Quaderno musicale di Annalibera" in her The twelve-tone compositions of Luigi Dallapiccola, 1960, p. 30-55).

Songs of imprisonment
 See his Canti di prigionia

Songs of liberation
 See his Canti di liberazione

Variations for orchestra
 See also his Quaderno musicale di Annalibera

674   Herz, Gerhard. "Current chronicle: Louisville, Kentucky," MQ
      41:79-85 (Jan 1955). Mus.
      A brief analysis of each variation.

                    WOLFGANG FORTNER

675   Stephan, Rudolf. "Gegenwärtiges Komponieren; Ein Überblick:
      Fortner, Pepping, Orff, Egk, Hartmann," Dt Univ Zt 6:12-15 (Sept
      28, 1951).
      A brief characterization of each composer's style.

See no. 703 (Stuckenschmidt, Hans Heinz. "Synthesis and new experiments:
      four contemporary German composers," Jul 1952).

676   Wörner, Karl H. "Wolfgang Fortner in seinen Werken seit 1945,"
      Schw MZ 93:260-263 (Jun 1953).
      Discussion of Fortner's works and style, 1945-1953.

See no. 151 ("Contemporary composers on their experiences of composi-
      tion with twelve notes: Wolfgang Fortner" in Rufer, Josef. Com-
      position with twelve notes, 1954, p. 181-183).

See no. 95 (Wörner, Karl H. Neue Musik in der Entscheidung, 1954,
      p. 101-104).

677   Laaff, Ernst. "Wolfgang Fortner," Melos 21:307-310 (Nov 1954).
      Port.
      List of works, p. 309-310. Brief summary of life and works.

678   Friedländer, Walther. "Moderner Kompositionsunterricht bei Wolf-
      gang Fortner an der nordwestdeutschen Musikakademie," NZfM
      116:113-114 (Nov 1955).
      Fortner as a teacher of composition.

679   Helm, Everett. "Six modern German composers," American-German
      review 23:12-15 (Dec 1956/Jan 1957).
         Wolfgang Fortner: p. 13-14; Hans Werner Henze: p. 14-15. Very
      brief summaries of style and works.

680   Driesch, Kurt. "Wolfgang Fortner: Zum fünfzigsten Geburtstag des
      deutschen Komponisten," Geist und Zeit [Düsseldorf], no. 6:119-124
      (1957).
      General discussion of life and works.

See no. 112 (Prieberg, Fred K. Lexikon der neuen Musik, 1958, p. 139-
    142).

See no. 116 (Vlad, Roman. Storia della dodecafonia, 1958, p. 146-147).

See no. 118a (Zillig, Winfried. "Neue Musik in Deutschland" in his Varia-
    tionen über neue Musik, 1959, p. 254-263).

Bluthochzeit

681 Fortner, Wolfgang. "Bluthochzeit nach Federico Garcia Lorca,"
     Melos 24:71-73 (Mar 1957). Illus.
     A description of the drama, by the composer.

Concerto, violin

682 Helm, Everett. "Current chronicle: Germany," MQ 38:606-610 (Oct
     1952). Mus.
     Brief summary; gives some themes and motives.

Fantasy for two pianos and orchestra on BACH

683 Helm, Everett. "Current chronicle: Germany," MQ 37:267-269 (Apr
     1951). Mus.
     Shows how Fortner treats the "BACH" motive throughout.

684 Engelmann, Hans Ulrich. "Fortners Phantasie über B-A-C-H,"
     Melos 21:131-135 (May 1954). Mus.
     Analysis, especially of serial and rhythmic aspects.

Impromptus

684a Dangel, Arthur. "Wolfgang Fortner [Impromptus]," Melos 27:79-84
     (Mar 1960) and 27:107-112 (Apr 1960). Mus.
     Serial analyses.

Kammermusik

See no. 213 (Unger, Udo. "Analyse von W. Fortners Fuge aus 'Kammer-
    musik,' komp. 1943" in his Die Klavierfuge im zwanzigsten Jahr-
    hundert, 1956, p. 91-92).

ROBERTO GERHARD

See no. 88 (Mitchell, Donald. "The emancipation of the dissonance," 1952,
    p. 144).

685 Mason, Colin. "Gerhard, Roberto" in Grove's Dictionary of music
     and musicians. 5th ed., London, Macmillan, 1954, v. 3:599-601.
     Includes a list of works (no bibliography).

See no. 151 ("Contemporary composers on their experiences of composition with twelve notes: Roberto Gerhard" in Rufer, Josef. Composition with twelve notes, 1954, p. 183-185).

686   Redlich, Hans Ferdinand. "Gerhard, Roberto" in Die Musik in
      Geschichte und Gegenwart. Kassel, Bärenreiter, 1955, v. 4, col.
      1786-1787.
         Includes a list of his works and a bibliography.

687   Drew, David. "Roberto Gerhard: the musical character," Score,
      no. 17:39-49 (Sept 1956). Mus.
         Biography and a discussion of his works.

See no. 163 (Gerhard, Roberto. "Developments in twelve-tone technique,"
      Sept 1956).

688   "Roberto Gerhard: catalog of works," Score, no. 17:54-60 (Sept 1956).

689   Vlad, Roman. "My first impressions of Roberto Gerhard's music,"
      Score, no. 17:27-38 (Sept 1056). Mus.
         Includes the score of the Capriccio movement of the String
         quartet. Discusses the general characteristics of Gerhard's
         music; analyzes his Symphony and String quartet.

See no. 116 (Vlad, Roman. Storia della dodecafonia, 1958, p. 137-144).

690   Mason, Colin. "A Spanish composer in exile," Listener 60:484
      (Sept 25, 1958).
         Brief survey of his life and works.

                        Concerto, violin

691   del Mar, Norman. "Gerhard as an orchestral composer," Score,
      no. 17:13-19 (Sept 1956). Mus.
         Analyses of his ballet suite, Don Quixote; Symphony, Homenaje
         a Pedrell; and Violin concerto.

                    Don Quixote (ballet suite)

See no. 691 (del Mar, Norman. "Gerhard as an orchestral composer,"
      Sept 1956).

                        The Duenna

692   Gardner, John. "The Duenna (1945-47)," Score, no. 17:20-26 (Sept
      1956). Mus.
         Synopsis of the story and a brief analysis of the music.

                 Homenaje a Pedrell (symphony)

See no. 691 (del Mar, Norman. "Gerhard as an orchestral composer,"
      Sept 1956).

See no. 689 (Vlad, Roman. "My first impressions of Roberto Gerhard's
      music," Sept 1956).

Quartet, string

See no. 689 (Vlad, Roman. "My first impressions of Roberto Gerhard's music," Sept 1956).

Symphony
See his Homenaje a Pedrell

JOSEF MATTHIAS HAUER

See no. 126 (Hauer, Josef Matthias. Vom Wesen des Musikalischen, 1923).

See no. 127 (Hauer, Josef Matthias. "Atonale Musik," Nov 1923).

See no. 129 (Hauer, Josef Matthias. Von Melos zur Pauke, 1925).

See no. 130 (Hauer, Josef Matthias. Zwölftontechnik, die Lehre von den Tropen, 1926).

693   Stuckenschmidt, Hans Heinz. "Josef Matthias Hauer," Musikblätter des Anbruch 10:245-249 (Aug/Sept 1928).
Discussion of his music and his theories.

694   Machabey, Armand. "La singulière figure de Jean-Mathias Hauer, musicien autrichien," Rev mus 12:221-233 (Mar 1931). Mus.
Discussion of his theories and his compositions.

695   Reich, Willi. "Josef Matthias Hauer," Die Musik 23:577-581 (May 1931). Mus., port.
Discussion of his theories and his compositions; includes a facsimile of a page of his Salambo.

See no. 137 (Eschman, Karl. Changing forms in modern music, 1945).

See no. 82 (Salazar, Adolfo. Music in our time, 1946).

See no. 83 (Schlee, Alfred. "Vienna since the Anschluss," Spring 1946).

See no. 297 (Bauer, Marion. "Schoenberg and his innovation" in her Twentieth century music, 1947, p. 207-230).

696   Schmale, Erich. "Die Zwölftonmusik von Josef Matthias Hauer," Schw MZ 88:305-306 (Jul 1948).
Brief bibliography, p. 306. An explanation of Hauer's system of tropes.

697   Eisenmann, Will. "Zur Sache Hauer," Schw MZ 88:353-354 (Sept 1948).
A reply to Schmale's article (see no. 696).

See no. 89 (Reich, Willi. "Versuch einer Geschichte der Zwölftonmusik" in Alte und neue Musik, 1952, p. 106-132).

See no. 27 (Pfrogner, Hermann. Die Zwölfordnung der Töne, 1953, p. 184-
    232).

698 Redlich, Hans Ferdinand. "Hauer, Josef (Matthias)" in Grove's
     Dictionary of music and musicians, 5th ed., London, Macmillan,
     1954, v. 4:135-137.
         Includes a list of works and a very brief bibliography.

See no. 153 (Searle, Humphrey. "Twelve-note music" in Grove's Diction-
    ary of music and musicians, 5th ed., London, Macmillan, 1954,
    8:617-623).

699 Mila, Massimo. "Lettera da Venezia," Rass mus 24:352 (Oct/Dec
     1954).
         Capsule résumé of Hauer's system of tropes.

See no. 196 (Perle, George. "The harmonic problem in twelve-tone
    music," Nov 1954).

700 Eimert, Herbert. "Hauer, Josef Matthias" in Die Musik in Geschichte
     und Gegenwart. Kassel, Bärenreiter, 1956. v. 5, col. 1823. Mus.
         Bibliography and list of works.

See no. 164 (Simbriger, Heinrich. "Die Situation der Zwölftonmusik,"
    Sept/Oct 1956).

701 Schwieger, Johannes. "Josef Matthias Hauer," ÖMZ 12:108-109 (Mar
     1957). Port.
         Brief discussion of the three periods, 1911, 1918, and 1920; his
         compositions are listed.

See no. 56 (Melichar, Alois. Musik in der Zwangsjacke, 1958).

See no. 112 (Prieberg, Fred K. Lexikon der neuen Musik, 1958, p. 185).

702 Wildgans, Friedrich. "Josef Matthias Hauer zum 75. Geburtstag,"
     ÖMZ 13:108-110 (Mar 1958). Port.
         Hauer's theories and works.

See no. 204a (Rochberg, George. "The harmonic tendency of the hexa-
    chord," Nov 1959).

HANS WERNER HENZE

703 Stuckenschmidt, Hans Heinz. "Synthesis and new experiments: four
     contemporary German composers," MQ 38:353-368 (Jul 1952), tr.
     by Abram Loft. Mus.
         German version in Schw MZ 93:1-10 (Jan 1953); Italian transla-
         tion in Rass mus 23:210-224 (Jul 1953).
         On Boris Blacher, Giselher Klebe, Wolfgang Fortner, and Hans
         Werner Henze (p. 364-368).

704   Bartlett, K. W. "Henze, Hans Werner" in Grove's Dictionary of
        music and musicians. 5th ed., London, Macmillan, 1954, v. 4:244-
        245.
        A list of his principal works is included.

See no. 679 (Helm, Everett. "Six modern German composers," Dec 1956/
        Jan 1957).

705   Stuckenschmidt, Hans Heinz. "Henze, Hans Werner" in Die Musik
        in Geschichte und Gegenwart. Kassel, Bärenreiter, 1957, v. 6, col.
        176-179. Mus.
        List of works; reproduction of part of autograph of König Hirsch.

706   Stuckenschmidt, Hans Heinz. "Hans Werner Henze: Porträt eines
        Komponisten," NZfM 118:491-492 (Sept 1957). Port.
        Discussion of works and style. Reprinted in the author's Schöpfer
        der neuen Musik (see no. 115, p. 290-301).

See no. 112 (Prieberg, Fred K. Lexikon der neuen Musik, 1958, p. 187-
        189).

See no. 168 (Stephan, Rudolf. "Hans Werner Henze" in Junge Komponisten,
        1958, p. 32-37 [Die Reihe, 4]).

See no. 116 (Vlad, Roman. Storia della dodecafonia, 1958, p. 148-150).

See no. 118a (Zillig, Winfried. "Neue Musik in Deutschland: Pepping,
        Genzmer, Fortner, Henze, Klebe" in his Variationen über neue
        Musik, 1959, p. 254-263).

707   Helm, Everett. "Current chronicle: Germany," MQ 45:241-248 (Apr
        1959). Mus.
        Includes biographical information and a discussion of his works
        and stylistic development.

708   Pauli, Hansjörg. "Hans Werner Henze's Italian music," Score, no.
        25:26-37 (Jun 1959). Mus.
        Discussion of his works since 1953.

                        König Hirsch

709   Rostand, Claude. "König Hirsch de H. Werner Henze," La table
        ronde [Paris], no. 109:157-158 (Jan 1957).
        A brief description.

710   Stuckenschmidt, Hans Heinz. "'König Hirsch' (Re Cervo) di Hans
        Werner Henze," Rass mus 27:153-155 (Jun 1957).
        A brief description.

HANNS JELINEK

711　Fiechtner, Helmut A. "Hanns Jelinek," Melos 20:242-245 (Sept 1953).
Port.
List of his works, p. 244-245. A brief biographical sketch and
discussion of his works and theories.

712　Krenek, Ernst. "Reviews of books," MQ 40:250-256 (Apr 1954).
Reviews Jelinek's Anleitung zur Zwölftonkomposition (see no.
190) and briefly discusses his compositional technique and his
works.

713　Wildgans, Friedrich. "Jelinek, Hanns" in Die Musik in Geschichte
und Gegenwart. Kassel, Bärenreiter, 1957, v. 6, col. 1847-1849.
Includes a list of his works and a brief bibliography.

See no. 112 (Prieberg, Fred K. Lexikon der neuen Musik, 1958, p. 221-
222).

713a Redlich, Hans F. "Hanns Jelinek," Mus rev 21:66-72 (Feb 1960).
Mus.
Brief discussion of his works and of his theory of twelve-tone
composition.

Symphonia brevis, op. 16

714　Blaukopf, Kurt. "Current chronicle: Austria," MQ 37:413-416 (Jul
1951). Mus.
His method of using the twelve-tone technique.

Zwölftonwerk, op. 15

715　Tenschert, Roland. "Hanns Jelinek; zu seinem 'Zwölftonwerk, op.
15,'" Schw MZ 91:452-454 (Nov 1951). Mus.
Brief biographical sketch; summary of dodecaphonic theories;
analysis of op. 15, particularly regarding serial technique. Review of Jelinek's book (see no. 190).

See no. 190 (Jelinek, Hanns. Anleitung zur Zwölftonkomposition nebst
allerlei Paralipomena, 1952).

See no. 151 ("Contemporary composers on their experiences of composition with twelve notes: Hanns Jelinek" in Rufer, Josef. Composition
with twelve notes, 1954, p. 186-188).

GISELHER KLEBE

See no. 703 (Stuckenschmidt, Hans Heinz. "Synthesis and new experiments:
four contemporary German composers," Jul 1952).

See no. 275 (Klebe, Giselher. "First practical work" in Electronic music,
1958, p. 17-18 [Die Reihe, 1]).

See no. 112 (Prieberg, Fred K. Lexikon der neuen Musik, 1958, p. 228-
229).

See no. 118a (Zillig, Winfried. "Neue Musik in Deutschland: Pepping,
Genzmer, Fortner, Henze, Klebe" in his Variationen über neue
Musik, 1959, p. 254-263).

Elegia appassionata (piano trio)

716   Mann, Robert W. "Vita musicale: Stoccolma," Rass mus 26:141-142
(Apr 1956).
Brief and general.

See no. 168 (Lewinsky, Wolf-Eberhard von. "Giselher Klebe" in Junge
Komponisten, 1958, p. 89-97 [Die Reihe, 4]).

Quartet, string, op. 9

See no. 703 (Stuckenschmidt, Hans Heinz. "Synthesis and new experiments:
four contemporary German composers," Jul 1952).

See no. 168 (Lewinsky, Wolf-Eberhard von. "Giselher Klebe" in Junge
Komponisten, 1958, p. 89-97 [Die Reihe, 4]).

Die Räuber

717   Klebe, Giselher. "Uber meine Oper 'Die Räuber,'" Melos 24:73-76
(Mar 1957). Mus.
"Grundform und dominierende Gestaltungsordungen; Charakteristik
der vier Hauptpersonen."

718   Helm, Everett. "Operas by Egk, Klebe, and Fortner," Mus rev
18:226-228 (Aug 1957).
Discussion of the libretto and the style of the music.

Die tödlichen Wünsche

719   Wörner, Karl H. "Current chronicle: Germany," MQ 46:80-83 (Jan
1960). Mus.
A review of Klebe's second opera. A piano reduction of the
Prelude (21 ms.) is included.

Trio, piano
See his Elegia appassionata

ERNST KRENEK

GENERAL

See no. 82 (Salazar, Adolfo. Music in our time, 1946).

720   Krenek, Ernst. Selbstdarstellung. Zürich, Atlantis [1948]. 66 p.
      Port.
          List of his compositions, p. 63-66. "Keine Selbstbiographie,
      sondern der Versuch einer Selbstanalyse." Last chapter re-
      printed as "Der musikalische Fortschnitt," Melos 16:71-75 (Mar
      1949). Port. (See no. 723.)

721   Krenek, Ernst. "Versuch einer Selbstanalyse: Vom 'Jonny' zur
      Zwölftonmusik," Melos 16:33-38 (Feb 1949).
          Krenek discusses the development of his compositional tech-
      nique in general terms.

See no. 88 (Mitchell, Donald. "The emancipation of the dissonance," 1952,
      p. 142-143).

722   Reich, Willi. "Ernst Krenek als Musikschriftsteller," Schw MZ
      [Ernst Krenek Heft] 93:113-114 (Mar 1953).
          A summary of Krenek's thought, as expressed in his writings.

723   Krenek, Ernst. "Self-analysis," New Mexico quarterly 23:5-57
      (Spring 1953). Mus., port.
          List of works, with opus number, year, and publisher, p. 51-56;
      discography, p. 56-57. "Revised and considerably enlarged ver-
      sion of a work originally published in German under the title,
      Selbstdarstellung." (See no. 720.)

See no. 151 ("Contemporary composers on their experiences of composi-
      tion with twelve notes: Ernst Krenek" in Rufer, Josef. Composition
      with twelve notes, 1954, p. 188-191).

See no. 95 (Wörner, Karl H. Neue Musik in der Entscheidung, 1954,
      p. 99-100).

724   Redlich, Hans Ferdinand. "Křenek, Ernst" in Grove's Dictionary
      of music and musicians. 5th ed., London, Macmillan, 1954, v. 4:
      844-848.
          Includes a bibliography and a list of his works.

725   Colucci, Matthew Joseph. A comparative study of contemporary
      musical theories in selected writings of Piston, Krenek, and Hinde-
      mith. [Ann Arbor, Mich., University Microfilms], 1957. 195 p.
      (University Microfilms, no. 23, 583.) (Thesis, Ph. D., music, Uni-
      versity of Pennsylvania.)
          Not seen; abstract in Dissertation Abstracts 17:2628 (1957).
      "Brief sketch of each composer's life; analysis of the musical
      theories."

726   Wörner, Karl H. "Krenek (Křenek), Ernst" in Die Musik in Ge-
      schichte und Gegenwart. Kassel, Bärenreiter, 1958, v. 7, col.
      1759-1763.
          Includes a list of his works.

See no. 118a (Zillig, Winfried. "Krenek, der Sucher" in his Variationen
über neue Musik, 1959, p. 236-239).

727   Saathen, Friedrich. "Ernst Křeneks Botschaft im Wort," Schw MZ
99:45-50 (Feb 1959).
Discusses Krenek's writings on music

GENERAL DESCRIPTIONS OF WORKS

728   Weissmann, Adolph. "Ernst Krenek," Modern music 6:17-23 (Nov/
Dec 1928).
An evaluation of Krenek's works through the late 1920's.

729   Preussner, Eberhard. "Ernst Krenek," Anbruch 11:154-159 (Apr
1929). Port.
Discussion of works and style.

730   Redlich, Hans Ferdinand. "Heimat und Freiheit: zur Ideologie der
jüngsten Werken Ernst Kreneks," Anbruch 13:54-58 (Feb 1930).
A discussion of his works.

731   Schneider, J. Marius. "Ernst Krenek," Rev mus 11:126-134 (Aug/
Sept 1930).
A survey of his works and style.

732   Günther, Siegfried. "Der Kurs in Ernst Kreneks jungstem Schaffen,"
Die Musik 23:587-592 (May 1931).
Krenek's works, op. 54-64; comparison with earlier works.

733   Erickson, Robert. "Krenek's later music (1930-1947)," Mus rev
9:29-44 (Feb 1948). Mus.
Emphasis on row technique. A list of Krenek's works, 1930-Jan
1947, p. 43-44.

See no. 721 (Krenek, Ernst. "Versuch einer Selbstanalyse," Feb 1949).

734   Reich, Willi. "Ernst Křeneks Arbeit in der Zwölftontechnik," Schw
MZ 89:49-53 (Feb 1949). Mus.
Krenek's serial technique, especially his use of "modes" (six-
note rows). Examples from his Sixth string quartet, his Lamentatio Jeremiae Prophetae, and his Sinfonischen Stück für Streich-
orchester.

735   Krenek, Ernst. "Kurzer Rechenschaftsbericht," Schw MZ 90:299-301
(Jun 1950).
The use of a modified twelve-tone technique in his works, 1939-
1950. Includes a list of his works of that period, p. 301.

736   Fiechtner, Helmut A. "Ernst Krenek," Musica 7:7-10 (Jan 1953).
Port.
Discussion of his works and of his various "periods" of com-
position. List of works, 1938-1952, p. 10.

737   Erickson, Robert. "Křeneks amerikanische texte," Schw MZ 93:104-108 (Mar 1953).
      Krenek's settings of English texts (Five prayers, Cantata for wartime, Santa Fé timetable, Tarquin, Dark waters, etc.).

738   Krenek, Ernst. "Zu meinem Kammermusikwerken 1936-1950," Schw MZ [Ernst Krenek Heft] 93:102-104 (Mar 1953).
      Primarily a discussion of row technique, in his Sixth and Seventh Quartets, Variations for piano, Sonatine for flute and clarinet, Sonata for viola solo, Lamentatio Jeremiae Prophetae, Third and Fourth Piano sonatas, and other chamber works.

See no. 155 (Ogdon, Wilbur Lee. Series and structure, 1955).

739   Joachim, Heinz. "Ernst Křenek," Schw MZ 95:1-5 (Jan 1955). Mus.
      Includes a list of his works, 1948-1954. Analysis of the first movement of his Sonata for violin and piano, 1944/45.

See no. 116 (Vlad, Roman. Storia della dodecafonia, 1958, p. 133-136, 270-271).

739a Krenek, Ernst. "Extents and limits of serial techniques," MQ [special issue on the Princeton Seminar in Advanced Musical Studies] 46:210-232 (Apr 1960). Diagrs., mus.
      The principles of serial rotation, indeterminacy, and other techniques, especially in Krenek's Lamentatio Jeremiae Prophetae; Kette, Kreis und Spiegel; Spiritus intelligentiae, sanctus; Sestina; and Sechs Vermessene.

INDIVIDUAL WORKS

Cantata, op. 72

See no. 526 (Bach, David Joseph. "New music by Berg, Webern, Krenek," Nov/Dec 1934).

Five prayers
      See his Prayers, Five

Five short pieces for strings
      See his Pieces for strings, Five

Invention for flute and clarinet

740   Schuh, Willi. "Zu Ernst Kreneks Invention," Schw MZ [Ernst Krenek Heft] 93:115 (Mar 1953). Mus.
      Includes a facsimile of the entire piece. This brief composition was written especially for the Schw MZ and is "ein einfaches Beispiel für die 'klassische' Reihentechnik." A short row analysis is given.

See no. 31 (Burkhard, Willy. "Versuch einer kritischen Auseinandersetzung mit der Zwölftontechnik," Mar 1954).

Kette, Kreis und Spiegel

741   Reich, Willi. "Musica-Bericht: Krenek und Martinu," Musica 12:161 (Mar 1958).
Very brief explanation of the row technique used.

See no. 739a (Krenek, Ernst. "Extents and limits of serial techniques," Apr 1960).

Lamentatio Jeremiae Prophetae

See no. 206 (Johnson, Martha. A study of linear design in Gregorian chant and music written in the twelve-tone technique, 1954).

See no. 52 (Rössler, Ernst Karl. "Zeitgenössische Kirchenmusik und christliche Gemeinde," Jan/Feb 1957).

742   Vellekoop, Gerrit. "De 'Lamentatio Jeremiae Prophetae' van Ernst Krsjenek," Mens en melodie 13:326-329 (Nov 1958). Mus.
Illustrates Krenek's use of hexachords.

See no. 739a (Krenek, Ernst. "Extents and limits of serial techniques," Apr 1960).

Pallas Athene weint

743   Koegler, Horst. "The international scene: Hamburg," Musical courier 152:27-28 (Nov 15, 1955). Illus.
Capsule description of the plot and the musical structure.

744   Joachim, Heinz. "Current chronicle: Germany," MQ 42:92-98 (Jan 1956). Mus.
General summation of Krenek's work and importance; the plot of the opera and the character of its music.

Pieces for strings, Five

See no. 46 (Kelterborn, Rudolf. "Stilistisch gegensätzliche Entwicklungen auf der Basis der Zwölftontechnik," Apr 1956).

Prayers, Five

745   Ogdon, Wilbur Lee. "The twelve-tone series and cantus firmus: a discussion of Ernst Krenek's 'Five Prayers,'" BAMS 11/13:86-88 (1948).
An abstract only.

Quartets, string
—no. 1

746 Evans, Edwin. "Krenek, Ernst" in Cobbett, Walter W. Cobbett's
cyclopedic survey of chamber music. London, Oxford University
Press, 1929/30, p. 76-79. Mus.
A brief description of the first and third String quartets.

—no. 3

See no. 746 (Evans, Edwin. "Krenek, Ernst," 1929/30).

—no. 6

See no. 484 (Leibowitz, René. "Les nouvelles générations de compositeurs
'dodécaphonistes' et leurs caractéristiques générales" in his Introduction à la musique de douze sons, 1949, p. 255-259).

Sestina

747 Krenek, Ernst. "Sestina," Melos 7/8:235-238 (Jul/Aug 1958). Mus.
A quite technical analysis by the composer. The complete poem
is quoted on p. 238.

See no. 739a (Krenek, Ernst. "Extents and limits of serial techniques,"
Apr 1960).

Sonata for violin and piano
—first movement

See no. 739 (Joachim, Heinz. "Ernst Křenek," Jan 1955).

Symphonic elegy

See no. 155 (Ogdon, Wilbur Lee. Series and structure, 1955, p. 162-231).

RENÉ LEIBOWITZ

See no. 141 ("Un musicien d'aujourd'hui: René Leibowitz" in Le système
dodécaphonique, 1949, p. 80-83 [Polyphonie, 4]).

See no. 29 (Goléa, Antoine. Esthétique de la musique contemporaine,
1954, p. 179-180).

748 Searle, Humphrey. "Leibowitz, René" in Grove's Dictionary of
music and musicians. 5th ed., London, Macmillan, 1954, v. 5:117.
Includes a list of his compositions and published theoretical
writings.

See no. 98 (Myers, Rollo H. "Music in France in the post-war decade,"
1954/55).

See no. 155 (Ogdon, Wilbur Lee. Series and structure, 1955).

Chamber symphony, op. 16

See no. 141 (Saby, Bernard. "Un aspect des problèmes de la thématique
sérielle; à propos de la Symphonie de chambre, op. 16, de René
Leibowitz" in Le système dodécaphonique, 1949, p. 54-63 [Poly-
phonie, 4]).

Quartets, strings
—no. 3

See no. 155 (Ogdon, Wilbur Lee. Series and structure, 1955).

Tourist death
(Air pour soprano et orchestre, op. 7)

See no. 484 (Leibowitz, René. "Les nouvelles générations de compositeurs
'dodécaphonistes' et leurs caractéristiques générales" in his Introduction à la musique de douze sons, 1949, p. 263-265).

BRUNO MADERNA

See no. 161 (Smith Brindle, Reginald. "The lunatic fringe, III: computational composition," Jul 1956).

See no. 105 (Smith Brindle, Reginald. "Italian contemporary music" in
Hartog, Howard, ed. European music in the twentieth century,
1957, p. 184, 185-186).

See no. 106 (Pestalozza, Luigi. "I compositori milanesi del dopoguerra,"
Mar 1957).

See no. 168 (Manzoni, Giacomo. "Bruno Maderna" in Junge Komponisten,
1958, p. 113-118 [Die Reihe, 4]).

See no. 112 (Prieberg, Fred K. Lexikon der neuen Musik, 1958, p. 263).

See no. 116 (Vlad, Roman. Storia della dodecafonia, 1958, p. 261-262).

749   Smith Brindle, Reginald. "Current chronicle: Italy," MQ 45:388-392
(Jul 1959). Mus.
       Brief description of his String quartet in two movements and
       his Serenata no. 2 for eleven instruments. Gives some bio-
       graphical background.

LUIGI NONO

See no. 29 (Goléa, Antoine. Esthétique de la musique contemporaine, 1954).

See no. 30 (Goléa, Antoine. "Deux portraits: Luigi Nono—Karlheinz Stockhausen" in La musique et ses problèmes contemporains, 1954, p. 112-114).

See no. 105 (Smith Brindle, Reginald. "Italian contemporary music" in Hartog, Howard, ed. European music in the twentieth century, 1957, p. 184, 186-187).

See no. 112 (Prieberg, Fred K. Lexikon der neuen Musik, 1958, p. 318-320).

See no. 116 (Vlad, Roman. Storia della dodecafonia, 1958, p. 264-265).

See no. 63 (Porena, Boris. "L'avanguardia musicale di Darmstadt," Sept 1958).

See no. 118a (Zillig, Winfried. "Die Jungen: Stockhausen, Boulez, Nono, Berio" in his Variationen über neue Musik, 1959, p. 190-199).

Il canto sospeso

750 Koegler, Horst. "The international scene: Germany," Musical courier 155:41 (Apr 1957).
       Very brief description.

See no. 170 (Stockhausen, Karlheinz. "Sprache und Musik" in Steinecke, Wolfgang, ed. Darmstädter Beiträge zur neuen Musik, 1958, p. 57-81).

See no. 168 (Unger, Udo. "Luigi Nono" in Junge Komponisten, 1958, p. 9-17 [Die Reihe, 4]).

Coro di Didone

751 Helm, Everett. "Current chronicle: Germany," MQ 45:101-102 (Jan 1959).
       A brief description.

Polifonica-Monodia-Ritmica

See no. 168 (Unger, Udo. "Luigi Nono" in Junge Komponisten, 1958, p. 9-17 [Die Reihe, 4]).

Varianti, for violin and orchestra

752 Kolisch, Rudolf. "Nonos Varianti," Melos 24:292-296 (Oct 1957).
       Mus.
       A short analysis; shows the use of permutation as a factor in composition.

HENRI POUSSEUR

753   "Henri Pousseur," Schw MZ 97:233 (Jun 1957).
      Very brief; gives biographical data and lists some of his works.

See no. 168 (Koenig, Gottfried Michael. "Henri Pousseur" in Junge Kom-
      ponisten, 1958, p. 18-31 [Die Reihe, 4]).

See no. 112 (Prieberg, Fred K. Lexikon der neuen Musik, 1958, p. 344-
      345).

See no. 166 (Pousseur, Henri. "Outline of a method" in Musical crafts-
      manship, 1959, p. 44-88 [Die Reihe, 3]).

See no. 637 (Metzger, Heinz-Klaus. "John Cage o della liberazione," Aug
      1959).

Impromptu for piano

See no. 166 (Pousseur, Henri. "Outline of a method" in Musical crafts-
      manship, 1957, 1959, p. 56-63 [Die Reihe, 3]).
      Includes a score of the work.

Quintet in memory of Webern

See no. 166 (Pousseur, Henri. "Outline of a method" in Musical crafts-
      manship, 1957, 1959, p. 48-55 [Die Reihe, 3]).

Scambi

754   Pousseur, Henri. "Scambi," Gravesaner Blätter, v. 4, no. 13:36-47
      (1959). Diagrs.
            English translation, p. 48-54. Details of the composition of
            Pousseur's electronic piece, Scambi.

See no. 71 (Eco, Umberto. "L'opera in movimento e la coscienza
      dell'epoca," Aug 1959).

Variations for piano

See no. 166 (Pousseur, Henri. "Outline of a method" in Musical crafts-
      manship, 1957, 1959, p. 64-88).

HUMPHREY SEARLE

755   Gorer, Richard. "An interim report on Humphrey Searle's music,"
      Mus sur 1:137-140 (1949). Mus.
            Brief outline of Searle's background and musical training; dis-
            cussion of his style and works. List of works, p. 140.

See no. 88 (Mitchell, Donald. "The emancipation of the dissonance," 1952,
      p. 144).

756   Mason, Colin. "Searle, Humphrey" in Grove's Dictionary of music
       and musicians. 5th ed., London, Macmillan, 1954, v. 7:679-681.
       Includes a list of his "principal compositions."

See no. 151 ("Contemporary composers on their experiences of composi-
       tion with twelve notes: Humphrey Searle" in Rufer, Josef. Compo-
       sition with twelve notes, 1954, p. 193-195).

757   Lockspeiser, Edward. "Humphrey Searle," MT 96:468-472 (Sept
       1955). Mus.
       Biographical sketch and discussion of works; list of composi-
       tions and writings, p. 472.

See no. 105 (Milner, Anthony. "English contemporary music" in Hartog,
       Howard, ed. European music in the twentieth century, 1957, p. 146-
       147).

See no. 112 (Prieberg, Fred K. Lexikon der neuen Musik, 1958, p. 398-
       399).

See no. 116 (Vlad, Roman. Storia della dodecafonia, 1958, p. 150-151).

                         Shadow of Cain

See no. 28 (Keller, Hans. "First performances and their reviews," Feb
       1953).

                         Sonata for piano

758   Keller, Hans. "First performances," Mus rev 13:43-44 (Feb 1952).
       An outline of the structure.

                    MÁTYÁS SEIBER

759   Weissmann, John S. "Mátyás Seiber: Style and technique," Listener
       55:476 (Mar 22, 1951).
       A brief survey of his works and method of using the twelve-tone
       technique.

See no. 88 (Mitchell, Donald. "The emancipation of the dissonance," 1952,
       p. 144).

760   Weissmann, John S. "Seiber, Mátyás (György)" in Grove's Diction-
       ary of music and musicians. 5th ed., London, Macmillan, 1954,
       v. 7:687-689.
       Includes a bibliography and catalog of his works.

See no. 151 ("Contemporary composers on their experiences of composi-
       tion with twelve notes: Mátyás Seiber" in Rufer, Josef. Composi-
       tion with twelve notes, 1954, p. 196-198).

761   Schweizer, Gottfried. "Komponistenporträt: Mátyás Seiber 50 Jahre," Musica 9:233-234 (May 1955). Port.
      Biographical data and brief characterization of Seiber's music.

762   Schweizer, Gottfried. "Zwischen Bartók und Schönberg: das Bild Mátyás Seibers," ZfM 116:269-272 (May 1955). Port.
      Influences on Seiber; brief discussion of works and style.

763   Keller, Hans. "Mátyás Seiber," MT 96:580-584 (Nov 1955). Mus.
      Biographical sketch; discussion of Seiber's row technique in some detail. List of published compositions, recordings, and writings, p. 583-584.

See no. 112 (Prieberg, Fred K. Lexikon der neuen Musik, 1958, p. 399-401).

See no. 116 (Vlad, Roman. Storia della dodecafonia, 1958, p. 151-153).

Quartets, string
—no. 1

764   Weissmann, John S. "Die Streichquartette von Mátyás Seiber," Melos 22:344-347 (Dec 1955) and 23:38-41 (Feb 1956). Mus.
      Tr. from the English by Willi Reich. Analyses of the first three quartets.

—no. 2

See no. 764 (Weissmann, John S. "Die Streichquartette von Mátyás Seiber," Dec 1955 and Feb 1956).

—no. 3
(Quartetto lirico)

765   Helm, Everett. "Current chronicle: Germany," MQ 41:521-524 (Oct 1955). Mus.
      A brief analysis of the form with some examples of the contrapuntal technique.

See no. 764 (Weissmann, John S. "Die Streichquartette von Mátyás Seiber," Dec 1955 and Feb 1956).

Ulysses

766   Carner, Mosco. "Mátyás Seiber and his Ulysses," Mus rev 12:105-112 (May 1951). Mus.
      A textual and musical analysis.

767   Seiber, Mátyás. "A note on 'Ulysses,'" Mus sur 3:263-270 (Jun 1951). Mus.
      The composer's description of the structure of his cantata.

KARLHEINZ STOCKHAUSEN

See no. 253 (Boulez, Pierre. "Tendances de la musique récente" in Vers une musique expérimentale, 1957, p. 28-35).

See no. 105 (Hartog, Howard. "German contemporary music" in his European music in the twentieth century, 1957, p. 201-202).

See no. 168 (Schnebel, Dieter. "Karlheinz Stockhausen" in Junge Komponisten, 1958, p. 119-133 [Die Reihe, 4]).

See no. 170a (Stephan, Rudolf. Neue Musik, 1958).

See no. 116 (Vlad, Roman. Storia della dodecafonia, 1958, p. 265-266).

768 Maegaard, Jan "Karlheinz Stockhausen," Nordisk Musikkultur 7:11-14 (Mar 1958). Port., mus.
       Discussion of Stockhausen's philosophy of composition and the characteristics, especially rhythmical, of his music.

See no. 636 (Maren, Roger. "The musical numbers game," Mar 6, 1958).

769 Manzoni, Giacomo. "Profili di musicisti contemporanei: Karlheinz Stockhausen," Musica d'oggi [new series] 1:229-233 (Apr 1958).
       A survey of his background and works.

See no. 63 (Porena, Boris. "L'avanguardia musicale di Darmstadt," Sept 1958).

770 Luening, Otto. "Karlheinz Stockhausen," Juilliard review 6:10-11 (Winter 1958/59). Port.
       A brief critical appraisal of Stockhausen and a chronological outline of the history of the Cologne group of electronic composers.

See no. 166 (Stockhausen, Karlheinz. ". . . how time passes . . ." in Musical craftsmanship, 1959, p. 10-40 [Die Reihe, 3]).

See no. 118a (Zillig, Winfried. "Die Jungen: Stockhausen, Boulez, Nono, Berio" in his Variationen über neue Musik, 1959, p. 190-199).

See no. 637 (Metzger, Heinz-Klaus. "John Cage o della liberazione," Aug 1959).

Gesang der Jünglinge

See no. 170 (Stockhausen, Karlheinz. "Sprach und Musik" in Steinecke, Wolfgang, ed. Darmstädter Beiträge zur neuen Musik, 1958, p. 57-81).

Gruppen für 3 Orchester

771 Stockhausen, Karlheinz. "Musik im Raum," Melos 25:317-320 (Oct 1958). Illus.
       Stockhausen's theories of music in space, particularly as worked out in his Gruppen für 3 Orchester; problems of concert hall design. (See no. 772.)

772   Stockhausen, Karlheinz. "Musik im Raum" in Berichte/Analysen.
      Wien, Universal Edition [c1959], p. 59-73. Illus. (Die Reihe, 5.)
          "Dieser Text diente als Vorlage für eine Vorlesung, die während
          der Internationalen Ferienkurse für Neue Musik 1958 in Darm-
          stadt gehalten wurde." (An expansion of no. 771; see also no. 174.)

773   Wörner, Karl H. "Current chronicle: Germany," MQ 45:237-239
      (Apr 1959).
          A brief description of the work.

Klavierstücke
−nr. 2

774   Mason, Colin. "Review of music," M & L 36:307-308 (Jul 1955).
          A brief review, including some discussion of rhythmic elements.

See no. 629 (Pestalozzi, Luigi. "Vita musicale: musiche nuovissime," Oct
      1956).
          Discusses the fifth, sixth, seventh, and eighth pieces.

−nr. 11

See no. 71 (Eco, Umberto. "L'opera in movimento e la coscienza
      dell'epoca," Aug 1959).

Komposition nr. 2

See no. 30 (Stockhausen, Karlheinz. "Une expérience électronique" in La
      musique et ses problèmes contemporains, 1954, p. 82-93).

See no. 170 (Nono, Luigi. "Die Entwicklung der Reihentechnik" in Stein-
      ecke, Wolfgang, ed. Darmstädter Beiträge zur neuen Musik, 1958,
      p. 25-37).

Kontrapunkten

775   Scherchen, Hermann. "Stockhausen und die Zeit: zur Geschichte
      einer Geschichte," Gravesaner Blätter, v. 4, no. 13:29-31 (1959).
          English translation, p. 32-34. Implications of changes made by
          Stockhausen in his Kontrapunkten.

Studie nr. 2

See no. 279 (Prieberg, Fred K. "Erste elektronische Partitur," Apr 1957).

Zeitmasse

See no. 170 (Nono, Luigi. "Die Entwicklung der Reihentechnik" in Stein-
      ecke, Wolfgang, ed. Darmstädter Beiträge zur neuen Musik, 1958,
      p. 25-37).

776   Pade, Else Marie, and Blyme, Anker. "Efter Stockhausen . . .,"
      Dansk musiktidsskrift 33:48-49 (Apr 1958).   Port.
          Review of Zeitmasse and discussion of Stockhausen's musical phil-
          osophy.

777 Helm, Everett. "Current chronicle: France," MQ 44:520-521 (Oct 1958).
The rhythmic structure is briefly discussed.

See no. 621 (Craft, Robert. "Boulez and Stockhausen," Nov 1958).

See no. 622 (Skulsky, Abraham. "After Webern, who?" Jan 1959).

IGOR STRAVINSKY

GENERAL

See no. 343 (Citkowitz, Israel. "Stravinsky and Schoenberg," Fall, 1954).

See no. 99 (Neighbor, Oliver. "The evolution of twelve-note music," 1954/1955).

778 Strawinsky in Amerika; das kompositorische Werk von 1939 bis 1955. Bonn, Boosey & Hawkes [c1955]. 87 p. Illus., mus. (Musik der Zeit; eine Schriftenreihe zur zeitgenössischen Musik, Heft 12.)
Partial contents: Lindlar, Heinrich, "Cantata" (Jan 1953), p. 30-34; Eimert, Herbert, "Die drei Shakespeare-Lieder (1953)," p. 35-38; Keller, Hans, "In Memoriam Dylan Thomas: Strawinskys Schönbergische Technik," p. 39-42 (from Tempo, Spring 1955; see no. 806); Craft, Robert, "Reihenkompositionen: vom 'Septett' zum 'Agon'" (Sept 1955), p. 43-54; list of works, 1939-55, p. 84-85.

See no. 160 (Perle, George. Serial composition and atonality, 1956).

See no. 348 (Burt, Francis. "An antithesis," Dec 1956 and Mar 1957).

779 Lindlar, Heinrich. Igor Strawinskys sakraler Gesang: Geist und Form der Christ-kultischen Kompositionen. Regensburg, Bosse Verlag, 1957. 93 p. Illus., mus. (Forschungsbeiträge zur Musikwissenschaft, Band 6.)
Partial contents: Cantata, p. 68-72; Shakespeare songs, p. 72-73; In Memoriam Dylan Thomas, p. 73; Canticum Sacrum, p. 74-79. (See nos. 787, 796.)

780 Le musiche religiose di Igor Strawinsky, con il catalogo analitico completo di tutte le sue opera. Venezia, Lombroso [1957]. 79 p. Illus., mus.
Contents: Piovesan, Alessandro, "Promesso," p. 5-9; Vlad, Roman, "Le musiche religiose di Strawinsky," p. 11-21; Craft, Robert, "Il 'Canticum sacrum,'" p. 23-36; Craft, Robert, "Bach-Strawinsky: Choral und Variationen über . . . 'Von Himmel hoch'. . ." p. 37-46; Piovesan, Alessandro, and Borri, Biancamaria, "Catalogo generale delle opere di Igor Strawinsky," p. 47-79.
The Craft articles first appeared under the title, "A concert for St. Mark" in Score, Dec 1956 (see no. 799).

781 Mason, Colin. "Stravinsky's contribution to chamber music," Tempo, no. 43:6-16 (Spring 1957). Mus.

Discussion of the Septet, In memoriam Dylan Thomas, and the
Shakespeare songs. A list of Stravinsky's chamber music, p. 15-
16. (See no. 787.)

782   Pfaundler, Geertruy von. "De jongste werken van Igor Strawinsky
(uit de jaren 1952-1957)," Mens en melodie 12:133-137 (May 1957).
Mus., port.
Discusses briefly the Canticum Sacrum, the Shakespeare songs,
and the Septet.

783   Gerhard, Roberto. "Twelve-note technique in Stravinsky," Score,
no. 20:38-43 (Jun 1957). Mus.
A description of Stravinsky's use of dodecaphonic elements. For
a German translation, see no. 787.

784   Stravinsky, Igor. "35 Antworten auf 35 Fragen," Melos 24:161-170
(Jun 1957). Port.
Translation, as "Answers to 34 [sic] questions; an interview
with Igor Stravinsky," Encounter, no. 46:3-7 (Jul 1957). Some of
the questions concern Stravinsky's serial technique.

785   Milner, Anthony. "Melody in Stravinsky's music," MT 98:370-371
(Jul 1957). Mus.
Very brief general article on the characteristics of Stravinsky's
melody; includes an illustration from the Canticum Sacrum.

786   Kirchmeyer, Helmut. Igor Strawinsky; Zeitgeschichte im Persön-
lichkeitsbild: Grundlagen und Voraussetzungen zur modernen Kon-
struktionstechnik. Regensburg, Gustav Bosse, 1958. xvi + 792 p.
Illus., mus. (Kölner Beiträge zur Musikforschung, Band 10.)
Contents: Erster Teil, "Die musik- und geistegeschichtliche
Stellung Igor Strawinskys"; Zweiter Teil, "Kritik und Polemic—
Dokumente zur Zeitgeschichte"; Dritter Teil, "Die Umgestaltung
des musikalischen Materials"; Vierter Teil, "Die Konstruktion:
Prinzipien der Konstruktion; Musiktheoretische Voraussetzungen;
Folgen der Konstruktion; Sonderformen der Konstruktion." Bibliography, p. 653-711 (general, not limited to Stravinsky); list of
works, p. 715-764 (very complete information, giving description,
instrumentation, names of sections, timing, publishers, recordings,
history of performances, etc., for each work).
An attempt to establish Stravinsky's place in the history of contemporary music. Much of the book is devoted to background
material, including Schoenberg and the development of the twelve-
tone technique.

See no. 112 (Prieberg, Fred K. Lexikon der neuen Musik, 1958, p. 405-
416).

787   Strawinsky: Wirklichkeit und Wirkung. Bonn, Boosey & Hawkes
[c1958]. 88 p. Illus., mus., ports. (Musik der Zeit: eine Schriftenreihe zu Musik und Gegenwart. Neue Folge, Heft 1.)
Partial contents: Gerhard, Roberto, "Die Reihentechnik des Dia-
tonikers," p. 18-22 (tr. by Alfred Becker from Gerhard's article
in Score; see nos. 783, 796); Lindlar, Heinrich, "Der Sakralkom-
ponist: Cantata/In memoriam Dylan Thomas, Canticum Sacrum/
Threni," p. 66-68 (from his Igor Strawinskys sakraler Gesang;

see no. 779); Mason, Colin, "Die Kammermusik," p. 72-81 (tr. by Alfred Becker from Mason's article in Tempo, see no. 781).

See no. 115 (Stuckenschmidt, Hans Heinz. "Igor Strawinsky" in his Schöp-fer der neuen Musik, 1958, p. 128-161).

See no. 116 (Vlad, Roman. "Strawinsky e la dodecafonia" in his Storia della dodecafonia, 1958, p. 161-174).

788   Füssl, Karl Heinz. "Selbstbesinnung am Beispiel Strawinskys," ÖMZ 13:461-466 (Nov 1958). Port.
      Primarily an article about Stravinsky's influence on the author, but with some discussion of the implications of Stravinsky's adaptation of serial techniques.

See no. 118a (Zillig, Winfried. "Strawinsky und das Zwölftonsystem" in his Variationen über neue Musik, 1959, p. 50-59).

SERIAL WORKS

Agon

789   Craft, Robert. "Ein Ballett für zwölf Tänzer," Melos 24:284-288 (Oct 1957). Mus.
      A brief formal analysis; the row technique is discussed in some detail.

790   Morton, Lawrence. "Current chronicle: Los Angeles," MQ 43:535-541 (Oct 1957). Mus.
      A brief analysis, with some examples of the row technique.

791   Vlad, Roman. "Vita musicale: Roma," Rass mus 27:322-324 (Dec 1957).
      A review, not an analysis.

See no. 116 (Vlad, Roman. "'Agon' di Strawinsky" in his Storia della dodecafonia, 1958, p. 329-338).

792   Lewkovitch, Bernhard. "Agon: Ballet for 12 dansere af Igor Stra-winsky," Nordisk musikkultur 7:89, 91, 93 (Oct 1958). Mus.
      An outline-analysis of the work.

793   Wouters, Jos. "Nieuwe balletmuziek van Strawinsky," Mens en melodie 13:301-306 (Oct 1958). Mus.
      The row, contrapuntal treatment, and rhythmic structure are discussed.

Canticum Sacrum ad Honorem Sancti Marci Nominis

794   Stein, Erwin. "Igor Stravinsky: Canticum Sacrum ad Honorem Sancti Marci Nominis," Tempo, no. 40:3-5 (Summer 1956).
      A very brief description, dealing with the over-all shape of the work and of its several sections.

795   Mila, Massimo. "Vita musicale: Venezia," Rass mus 26:204-206
       (Jul 1956).
       A review, not an analysis.

796   Lindlar, Heinrich. "Strawinskys sakraler Gesang," NZfM 117:548-
       552 (Oct 1956). Diagrs.
       Parallels between the structure of the Canticum Sacrum and
       that of the Basilica of St. Mark in Venice. (See also nos. 779,
       787.)

797   Swarowsky, Hans. "Canticum Sacrum," ÖMZ 11:399-405 (Nov 1956).
       Mus.
       A description, with some row analysis.

798   Schuh, Willi. "Uraufführungen neuer Kirchenmusik: Strawinskys
       'Canticum Sacrum,'" Musik und Kirche 26:296-298 (Nov/Dec 1956).
       Reprinted from the Neue Züriche Zeitung (Fernausgabe), nr.
       257, Sept 18, 1956. A fairly detailed description of the work's
       structure.

799   Craft, Robert. "A concert for Saint Mark," Score, no. 18:35-45 (Dec
       1956). Mus., port.
       Italian translation in Le musiche religiose di Igor Strawinsky,
       no. 780. Analyses of the Canticum Sacrum and the Von Himmel
       Hoch variations.

800   Rostand, Claude. "Canticum Sacrum d'Igor Strawinsky," La table
       ronde [Paris], no. 109:155-157 (Jan 1957).
       Review and general brief description.

801   Weissmann, John S. "Current chronicle: Italy," MQ 43:104-110 (Jan
       1957). Mus.
       Survey of the structure as a whole; aesthetic implications.

802   Winter, Carl. "Canticum Sancti Marci: Strawinskys neues geist-
       liches Chorwerk," Musica sacra 77:8-17 (Jan 1957). Mus., port.
       Gives an outline of the form and a general description of each
       section.

See no. 782 (Pfaundler, Geertruy von. "De jongste werken van Igor Stra-
       winsky," May 1957).

803   Andriessen, Hendrik. "Het 'Canticum Sacrum' van Strawinsky,"
       Mens en melodie 12:285-289 (Sept 1957). Mus.
       A discussion of the structure.

804   Reck, Albert von. "Gestaltzusammenhänge in 'Canticum Sacrum'
       von Strawinsky: Tonalität und Form," Schw MZ 98:49-68 (Feb 1958).
       Diagrs., mus.
       An elaborate structural analysis.

Double canon for string quartet

See his Movements for piano and orchestra

Epitaphium für das Grabmal des
Prinzen Max Egon zu Fürstenburg
See his Movements for piano and orchestra

In Memoriam Dylan Thomas

805   Turchi, Guido. "Letture critiche: Igor Strawinsky—In memoriam
Dylan Thomas," Riv mus ital 57:69-72 (Jan/Mar 1955).
Philosophical considerations, not an analysis. Rather negative
review.

806   Keller, Hans. "In memoriam Dylan Thomas: Stravinsky's Schoen-
bergian technique," Tempo, no. 35:13-20 (Spring 1955). Mus.
"The present article is no more than an illustration appended
to my analytic music example of the complete central song [p.
16-20]." The analysis is indicated on the score. (German translation in no. 778.) (See also no. 807.)

807   Shawe-Taylor, Desmond. "The arts and entertainment: Stravinsky
as serialist," New statesman and nation [ser. 2] 50:12-13 (Jul 2,
1955).
An answer to Keller's analysis (see no. 806); a reply by Keller
in New statesman and nation [ser. 2] 50:72 (Jul 16, 1955).

808   Keller, Hans. "A serial masterpiece," Mus rev 16:342-344 (Nov
1955). Diagr.
A brief serial and thematic analysis.

809   Goldman, Richard F. "Current chronicle: New York," MQ 42:236-
239 (Apr 1956). Mus.
Illustrates some of the canonic techniques; claims that the piece
is "augenmusik."

See no. 781 (Mason, Colin. "Stravinsky's contribution to chamber music,"
Spring 1957).

Movements for piano and orchestra

809a Mason, Colin. "Stravinsky's newest works," Tempo, no. 53/54:2-10
(Spring/summer 1960), mus.
Serial analysis of the Movements; also brief analyses of two
miniature works, the Double canon for string quartet and the
Epitaphium.

809b Goldman, Richard F. "Current chronicle: New York," MQ 46:260-
264 (Apr 1960).
A brief description of the Movements and also of the Double
canon for string quartet.

809c Briner, Andreas. "Guillaume de Machaut 1958/59, oder Strawinskys
'Movements for piano and orchestra,'" Melos 27:184-186 (Jun 1960).
Mus.
A brief analysis.

Septet

810   Stein, Erwin. "Stravinsky's Septet (1953) . . . an analysis," Tempo,
        no. 31:7-10 (Spring 1954). Mus., illus.
        A formal analysis.

811   [Keller, Hans]. "First performances: Schönbergians and Stravin-
        skyians," Mus rev 15:307-310 (Nov 1954).
        Aesthetic considerations.

812   Redlich, Hans. "New music: a critical interim report," Mus rev
        16:167-168 (May 1955). Mus.
        Brief example of "thematic integration" in the work.

813   Schilling, Hans Ludwig. "Zur Instrumentation in Igor Strawinskys
        Spätwerk aufgezeigt an seinem 'Septett 1953,'" Archiv für Musik-
        wissenschaft 13:181-196 (1956). Mus.
        A discussion of the instrumentation only.

See no. 781 (Mason, Colin. "Stravinsky's contribution to chamber music,"
        Spring 1957).

See no. 782 (Pfaundler, Geertruy von. "De jongste werken van Igor Stra-
        winsky," May 1957).

Shakespeare songs

See no. 778 (Eimert, Herbert. "Die drei Shakespeare-Lieder (1953)" in
        Strawinsky in Amerika, 1955, p. 35-38 [Musik der Zeit, 12]).

See no. 781 (Mason, Colin. "Stravinsky's contribution to chamber music,"
        Spring 1957).

See no. 782 (Pfaundler, Geertruy von. "De jongste werken van Igor Stra-
        winsky," May 1957).

Threni, id est Lamentationes
Jeremiae Prophetae

814   Pauli, Hansjörg. "On Stravinsky's 'Threni,'" Tempo, no. 49:16-33
        (Autumn 1958). Mus.

        _____. "Zur seriellen Struktur von Igor Strawinskys 'Threni,'"
        Schw MZ 98:450-456 (Dec 1958). Mus.
        Detailed analysis of the textual and musical structure.

815   Mila, Massimo. "Vita musicale: Venezia; I 'Threni' di Strawinsky,"
        Rass mus 28:215-217 (Sept 1958).
        General description and aesthetic discussion; not an analysis.

816   Ruppel, K. H. "Berichte aus dem Ausland; Strawinskys neues Werk:
        'Threni,'" Melos 25:369-371 (Nov 1958).
        Brief account of Stravinsky's road to serial technique; general
        description of the work.

817   Smith Brindle, Reginald. "Reports from abroad: Venice Contempo-
        rary Music Festival," MT 99:619-620 (Nov 1958).
        Very brief review.

818   Glock, William. "The arts and entertainment: Stravinsky's Threni,"
      New statesman 56:723-724 (Nov 22, 1958).
      A brief description and evaluation.

819   Schuh, Willi. "Strukturanalyse eines Fragments aus Strawinskys
      'Threni,'" Schw MZ 98:456-460 (Dec 1958). Mus.
      Analysis of the first section (ms. 322-342) of the "Solacium"
      from the third part of Threni, "De elegia tertia."

820   Weissmann, John S. "Current chronicle: Italy," MQ 45:104-110 (Jan
      1959). Mus.
      Brief analytical description, including row technique.

821   Vlad, Roman. "Igor Strawinskys 'Threni,'" Melos 26:36-39 (Feb
      1959). Mus.
      A brief description of the row technique and the general form.

822   Weissmann, John S. "The new in review; Venice 1958: Stravinsky's
      Threni," Mus rev 20:74-76 (Feb 1959). Mus.
      A brief description.

823   Lewkovitch, Bernhard. "Stravinskijs klagensange," Dansk musiktids-
      skrift 34:37-40 (Mar 1959). Mus.
      A brief description.

AUTHOR INDEX

Brauner, Rudolph Franz. Von Drei-
klang zum Zwölftonakkord, 188
Brindle, Reginald Smith, see Smith
Brindle, Reginald
Briner, Andreas. Guillaume de
Machaut 1958/59, oder Strawin-
skys 'Movements for piano and
orchestra,' 809c
Broch, Hermann. Irrationale Er-
kenntnis in der Musik, 293
Bruno, Anthony. Two American
twelve-tone composers: Milton
Babbitt and Ben Weber, 602
Bruyn, J. W. de. Electronic music,
281
Bücken, Ernst. Führer und Prob-
leme der neuen Musik, 310
Burkhard, Willy. Versuch einer
kritischen Auseinandersetzung
mit der Zwölftontechnik, 31
Burnier, Lucien. Réflexions sur la
dodécaphonie, 16
Burt, Francis. An antithesis, 348
Busoni, Ferrucio Benvenuto. Entwurf einer neuen Asthetik der
Tonkunst, 1

Cage, John. Experimental music,
635; To describe the process of
composition used in 'Music for
piano 21-52,' 166; Zur Geschichte
der experimentellen Musik in den
Vereinigten Staaten, 174
Calvocoressi, M. D. The classicism
of Arnold Schönberg, 308
The Canon [Schoenberg Jubilee
issue], 300
Carner, Mosco. Alban Berg, 522;
Mátyás Seiber and his Ulysses,
766; Technique of twelve-note
music, 120
Les carnets critiques, 611
Carsalade du Pont, Henri de. La
musique dodécaphoniste, 102
Castiglioni, Niccolò. Sul rapporto
tra parola e musica nella seconda
Cantata di Webern, 594; Il valore
del silenzio e della durata, 58
Catalogue des oeuvres d'Arnold
Schoenberg, 406
Cecci, César. Qué es la dodeca-
fonía, 125

Chailley, Jacques. Malentendus sur
le mot 'atonalité,' 23; Traité historique d'analyse musicale, 145
Chambure, Alaine de. Infrastructure
technique, 267
Chase, Gilbert. America's music,
99a
Citkowitz, Israel. Stravinsky and
Schoenberg, 343
Clarke, Henry Leland. The abuse of
the semitone in twelve-tone music,
175
Collaer, Paul. Le cas Schoenberg,
314; La musique moderne, 1905-
1955, 100; Une nouvelle oeuvre
d'Alban Berg: Loulou, 525
Colucci, Matthew Joseph. A comparative study of contemporary
musical theories in selected
writings of Piston, Krenek, and
Hindemith, 725
Cort Van den Linden, R. Arnold
Schoenberg, 312
Costarelli, Nicola. Nota sulla dodecafonia, 119
Costère, Edmond. Entre l'harmonie
classique et les harmonies contemporaines, 193
Cowell, Henry. Current chronicle:
New York (Jan 1949), 456; ____
(Jan 1952), 617, 632
Craft, Robert. Anton Webern, 591;
Bach-Strawinsky, 780; Ein Ballett für zwölf Tänzer, 789; Boulez and Stockhausen, 621; Il 'Canticum sacrum,' 780; A concert
for Saint Mark, 799; Discoveries
and convictions, 576; Reihenkompositionen: vom 'Septett' zum
'Agon,' 778; Schoenberg's Erwartung, 429
Curjel, Hans. Cage oder das wohlpräparierte Klavier, 634

Dace, Wallace. The dramatic structure of Schönberg's Erwartung,
430
Dahlhaus, Carl. Eine 'dritte Epoche'
der Musik? 227
Dallapiccola, Luigi. A propos d'un
trait 'expressionniste' de Mozart,
141; Contemporary composers on

SUBJECT INDEX

Underlined items are main subject entries.